C

S.

D0378228

JUNGLE TRAVEL
& SURVIVAL

JUNGLE TRAVEL & SURVIVAL

John Walden

THE LYONS PRESS
Guilford, Connecticut
An Imprint of The Globe Pequot Press

Dedicated to the tribal peoples of the great tropical forests of Amazonia who have allowed me the pleasure of their company.

The Lyons Press is an imprint of The Globe Pequot Press.

Printed in Canada

The Library of Congress Cataloging-in-Publication Data is available on file.

Publisher's Note

This book is meant to provide authoritative emergency medical and first aid information to those venturing into the jungle. It should not be used as a substitute for professional advice or training. The author and publisher disclaim any responsibility for problems that may occur as a result of following the information, procedures, or techniques included in the work.

CONTENTS

THRIVING ON THE TRAIL

MEDICAL CONCERNS IN THE TROPICS

ACKNOWLEDGMENTS

I am greatly indebted to Paul Auerbach, whose editorial talents made possible the shortened, more-to-the-point version of "Jungle Travel and Survival," which appears as a chapter in the fourth edition of his book, *Wilderness Medicine*. For anyone seriously interested in all aspects of wilderness medicine and survival, Paul's encyclopedic text is essential reading.

Also, thank you to: Tawnya Bolt, Mark Bracker (many chapters in this book had their origin in lectures I prepared for the Wilderness Medicine Conference, which is held annually in Snowmass, Colorado, under the direction of Mark Bracker and Terry Davidson), Chuck Clements, Murray Corman, John Cornell, Richard Crespo, Terry Davidson (for advice on snake envenomation), Ken Devlin, Dodge Engleman, Dan Evans (a good friend and traveling companion on several trips into the eastern lowlands of Ecuador; a more passionate and dedicated teacher of ethnobotany one will not find anywhere), Nick Freiden, Mark Greenberg (Mark's photos have graced the pages of everything from *People* magazine to *Life*; like all pros, he makes it look easy), Ron Guderian, Peter Hackett, Richard Hatcher, Steve Hoffman, Charles Houston, James Leiffrig, Bev McCoy (any hint of literary talent on these pages is most likely the result of Bev's hours of scrutiny and stylistic changes), Steve Petrany, Tweed Roosevelt (for the non-stop laughs and friendship during and after the 1992 Rio Roosevelt

Expedition), Tom Rushton, Glenn Schnepf, Brando Skyhorse (who took the first draft and somehow made what I actually meant to say come through), Tracey Smith, Michael Stuart (President of Amazonia Foundation, Michael has done much to make a difference in the lives of indigenous peoples in Amazonas State, Venezuela), Bob Walker, and Ted Williams (with assistance from Nikki for the illustrations).

JUNGLE TRAVEL: AN INTRODUCTION

I am unaware of any work—prior to this publication—devoted solely to the conditions encountered in the tropical rainforest and that features strategies for successful trips into such zones. Throughout *Jungle Travel and Survival*, I have attempted to take a straightforward, nuts-and-bolts approach: tell the reader what works and what doesn't.

Readers who choose to take the "quick and dirty" approach and simply want to know what equipment to consider for purchase and what essential skills they need for success will find the chapters on general preparations, gear, coping with the jungle environment, jungle trekking, and camp life of particular interest. A discussion of essential immunizations for overseas travel appears in the chapter on medical preparations. Because travelers' diarrhea is so common and malaria is such a potentially lethal disease, I strongly recommend readers pay careful attention to those chapters. Personal health risks due to environmental factors are covered in the chapter titled hazards.

Unfamiliar cultures and environments are covered in cultural and psychologic factors. There are also chapters on the dynamics of group travel in exotic environments, women in the jungle, and traveling with children in the tropics. A selective overview of what makes the rainforest tick can be found in the chapter on the tropical environment.

A portion of this book is devoted to infectious diseases, which features a number of diseases, some exotic, that may pose a health threat to travelers. As a physician specializing in clinical tropical medicine, I confess I included some obscure diseases only because they are so downright outlandish! However, I have made every effort to avoid medical jargon and discuss specific diseases in plain English.

The section on survival strategies acknowledges that wilderness adventure in minimally explored jungle involves risk. This chapter discusses ways to increase one's chances of getting out alive in an emergency.

Strictly speaking, the term "jungle" refers to land overgrown with tangled vegetation. In this book, I have chosen to use "jungle" interchangeably with "rainforest" because 1) most people are familiar with the term, and 2) jungle evokes the spirit of wildness that is integral to the rainforest experience.

For 35 years I have had the pleasure of traveling in the company of tribal peoples in the vast jungle regions of Amazonia. Through the curious intertwining of our lives, I have come to know a part of the world where peak experiences seem to be the rule, not the exception, and where, frankly, I feel most alive. These experiences have in turn led me on philosophical journeys that have changed my own worldview considerably. By reading this book, you will learn the basics of preparing for travel in the tropical rainforest. Perhaps, too, through these pages you will embark on philosophical journeys of your own.

PREPARING FOR THE JUNGLE

GENERAL PREPARATIONS
Trip Planning
Conditioning
Readings

MEDICAL PREPARATIONS
Health and Safety Information Prior to Travel
Locating Physicians For Predeparture and
    Posttrip Consultation
Travelers' Medical Insurance and Emergency
    Medical Transport
Immunizations and Other Preventive Measures
Medical Kit

GEAR
Footwear
Clothing
Bedding
Backpacks
Other Useful Items
Photography

1

GENERAL PREPARATIONS

Trip Planning
Conditioning
Readings

Persons who venture into the tropical rainforest step into an exotic and mysterious environment that can be unforgiving. Preparedness makes the difference between misery and pleasure.

You should know the truth up front: on my first dozen or so trips into the tropical rainforest, I made every single mistake in the book. To this day, when the Chachi Indians of Ecuador call their children and grandchildren over to meet me, they don't introduce me as the person who brought medicine and a vaccine that reduced the incidence of tuberculosis in the area—oh, no. They say, "This is the imbecile who thought he could camp on a sandbar in the Cayapa River during the height of the rainy season!"

Luckily, I survived long enough to begin to understand how much I had to learn. I also had the sense to recognize that my traveling companions, indigenous peoples born and reared in the great forests of Amazonia, knew *everything* about survival in the jungle environment. By trusting their judgment implicitly and copying their behaviors on the trail, I began to develop the skills that have made my travels today safer and rewarding.

Of course, there are those who aren't so lucky.

Kent, a 40-year-old computer whiz, volunteered to work on a storage building at a mission outpost in Ecuador. The trip down was uncomfortable, and, as a result, he found himself starting his 3- to 4-

hour trek with about one hour's sleep, after a day in which he had eaten little and drunk a cup of coffee, half a can of Pepsi, and maybe one full glass of water.

"I got in trouble right off the bat," he recalls. He agreed to carry a friend's tripod in addition to his own backpack, and even ran up a little hill with him at the start of the hike to get a photo of the group. "I was sweating buckets even before we were 200 yards out of the village," he said.

Kent was wearing jeans, a medium-weight synthetic shirt, and tennis shoes. As he slid around on the muddy trail, he noticed he was working twice as hard as others who wore shoes with a decent tread. The jeans became waterlogged immediately, adding considerable weight and restricting movement; the shirt created a sweat-lodge environment for his upper body. "About one hour into the hike I felt nauseated and dizzy and had one heck of a headache," he said. "It felt like I was coming down with the flu."

When others realized that Kent was falling behind, staggering and disoriented, they took steps that probably saved his life: they poured water over his head and trunk, fanned him, and plopped him down in the relatively cool waters of a creek. They also forced him to drink 3 full quarts of water.

Kent had reached the point of heat exhaustion and was just short of full-blown heat stroke—a condition he would not have survived. So what happened?

Kent was poorly prepared for a trek in the rainforest. He had not acclimated (it takes 4 to 5 days for minimally acceptable acclimatization); he was physically exhausted even before he hit the trail; he was wearing improper footwear and clothes; he was carrying far too much gear from the standpoint of weight; and, most important, he consumed only a fraction of the liquids he needed to replace the 2 gallons or so he lost on the trail that day, as well as the fluid lost when he didn't maintain adequate hydration on the day before the trek.

To make sure that what happened to Kent doesn't happen to you, let's start by discussing key areas that are essential to a successful journey.

TRIP PLANNING

Where to Begin

I always recommend that beginners start their jungle adventures in the structured setting of small-group travel with one of the many reputable tour companies scattered throughout tropical regions of the world. First-class tourist agencies employ knowledgeable guides and assistants who can dramatically enhance your first-time jungle experience. Why struggle to get the basics down pat through trial and error when you can learn the tricks of the trade from pros? In the Americas, three countries—Costa Rica, Ecuador, and Peru—have a long history of catering to ecology-minded jungle travelers.

Finding a Reputable Tour Company/Guide

Reliable tour companies and guides can be found in standard guidebooks or on the Internet.

South American Explorers (*www.samexplo.org*) provides reliable, up-to-date information on commercial trips into jungle regions throughout South America. Member services in South American Explorers include: trip planning; discounts on maps, guidebooks, trips, schools; and e-mail, fax, and storage at Clubhouses in Quito, Ecuador, and in Lima and Cusco, Peru. This nonprofit organization is great for networking and bringing like-minded people together.

Expeditions

Once you get into the areas of exploration and high-risk expedition travel, the issue becomes one of finding a competent leader/organizer. If you are about to sign up as a member of a group trek, and you have reason to question the qualifications and experience of the group leader(s), ask the impolite questions early and boldly; get independent confirmation of the group leader's past successes and experience. It is better to get the bad news while you have time to bail out.

CONDITIONING

Certain people, particularly those with habitually sedentary lifestyles, may be reluctant to consider a jungle outing because of the notion that you must be supremely fit to survive on the trail. This simply is not so—there are plenty of jungle adventures available to those who are not in the pink of youth and fitness. On the other hand, a 2- to 3-week nonstop trek across previously unexplored tracts in Brazil obviously demands some degree of conditioning and skill.

Ideal Weight

Indigenous peoples in jungle regions are almost always slender. After trekking with large numbers of nonindigenous men and women in equatorial regions, I have observed that overweight or powerfully built individuals, particularly men, seem to fare the worst, especially with heat-related illness. Getting down to your ideal weight pays off on the trail.

Leg Strength

Good leg strength, acquired by training with a stair-climbing exercise machine, offers appropriate preparation. Three to four months of 1-hour workouts 3 times each week should do the trick. I find the elliptical motion of Precor or StairMaster trainers ideal and less likely to reactivate old problems with a trick knee.

Balance

On frequently used trails, natives often place a single log across creeks, ravines, and swampy areas. These log "bridges" may be up to 20 feet high and 75 feet long. Since there is generally nothing to hold on to, good balance is essential. Walking on the rails of train tracks or on curbs may help in preparation. An even better activity is to go to the woodlands and practice walking on logs.

Head stability is important. Equilibrium can be enhanced by avoiding brisk head movements and by employing the "gaze-anchoring" technique of tightrope walkers: fix the gaze on a spot near the end of the log and do not stare down at the spot just ahead of the feet. Covel Ice Walker Quick Clip Cleats, available from REI (see section on gear on page 23) should also be considered for crossing particularly intimidating log bridges that are long, slippery, and high off the ground.

It is particularly risky to attempt to cross dangerous single-log bridges with a backpack; the slightest asymmetrical, unaccustomed load on your back will throw off your balance. It is possible to improve balance by practicing for several weeks with a pack on your back in the woods at home, but it is always best to have a porter carry heavy items across hazardous log bridges. If a porter is not handy, do what I do: straddle the log and scoot across on your fanny! You may look silly, but at least you are unlikely to slip off the log and suffer serious injury.

Acclimatization

When planning your trip, set aside at least 4 days to allow for acclimatization before beginning a strenuous long-distance trek. Little acclimatization is required for jungle outings that are limited to 1 to 3 hours of guided birdwatching or plant identification along a well-marked nature trail.

Techniques that facilitate acclimatization to heat and humidity and suggestions for preventing heat-related illness are fully discussed in Chapter 7.

Using a Machete

Because we all grew up watching jungle-adventure movies, it is only natural that first-time travelers to the rainforest imagine that much of their day will be spent hacking through dense foliage. In fact, the machete is seldom used to clear a path through the forest; natives generally hike through areas that are naturally free of pesky undergrowth, or they follow trails that were cleared long ago. More commonly, the machete is used to cut off the occasional spiny leaf or branch that has grown onto the trail, secure a tropical fruit, or cut poles, leaves and vines needed to make a shelter. As noted in Chapter 8, an experienced individual should be in charge of transporting and using the machete. If you plan to use a machete yourself, buy a good one (check the gear section) and practice using it in the woods at home.

A curious aside: Women, I've observed, only use machetes to actually do something purposeful. I've long noticed that indigenous men walk down the trail lopping off branches and twigs at random. They seem to use the machete to slice tendrils and other greenery in the same way some of us twiddle our fingers—just something to pass the time. Must be a guy thing . . .

READINGS

I wouldn't think of going into any out-of-the-way place without first familiarizing myself, through reading, with the human inhabitants and ecosystems of that particular region. I consider pretrip reading as critical as physical conditioning. Through selective reading, you will be able to make more informed decisions and minimize cultural gaffes. When traveling in areas populated by tribal peoples, it is critical to become as fully informed as possible to avoid the societal taboos that litter the landscape.

There is another reason to prepare yourself through selective readings. The beauty of the jungle speaks for itself, but you will have a much greater appreciation for what you are seeing and thus *feeling*, if you have some basic understanding of the peoples, places, flora, fauna, and ecosystems of the tropical forest.

People and Places

Back issues of *National Geographic* magazine provide an excellent introduction to the people and places the traveler plans to visit. *The Complete National Geographic* on CD-ROM contains 182,000 spectacular photographs, 9,400 articles, and every page map that has appeared over the past 110 years. The search engine of this reasonably priced product allows the user to search by keyword, title, subject, or contributor. *The Emerald Realm,* a National Geographic Society special publication, also offers a superb general overview of the world's tropical forests. Contributors to *National Geographic* also usually have written extensively on their subject, often in book form.

People of the Tropical Rain Forest, edited by Denslow and Padoch, contains 22 essays on the peoples of the world's rainforests, emphasizing South America, tropical Asia, and, to a lesser degree, Africa. Readers who wish to acquire in-depth knowledge of peoples and customs should consult recognized reference works. The incomparable seven-volume *Handbook of South American Indians* remains the standard on South American ethnology. The UNESCO, *General History of Africa* series is an ambitious academic account of the ideas, civilization, societies, and traditions of the continent's peoples.

The CIA World Factbook (*www.odci.gov/cia/publications/factbook/*) includes geographic, political, economic, and demographic information on specific countries.

Flora, Fauna, and Ecosystems

John Kricher's *A Neotropical Companion* is an excellent introduction to the animals, plants, and ecosystems of the New World tropics. Kricher, a professor of biology at Wheaton College, has extracted useful information from a broad range of sources on the natural history of the Neotropics to produce a book that is educational and deliciously entertaining. Though slanted toward the jungles of Central and South America, the basic themes are universal and will well serve readers contemplating a trip to any tropical or subtropical region of the world. Forsyth and Miyata's highly acclaimed *Tropical Nature* is guaranteed to stimulate curiosity about tropical forests. Both *A Neotropical Companion* and *Tropical Nature* are suitable for a broad audience.

Ethnobotany

Readers wanting to delve into the fascinating scientific and anthropologic literature of the ubiquitous use of hallucinogens among indigenous populations should check out the splendid writings of Richard Evans Schultes. Photographic essays by Schultes, such as *Vine of the Soul,* and a companion work, *Where the Gods Reign,* offer delightful illuminations into that which is both mundane and sacred in the life of Amerindians. *Plants of the Gods,* coauthored with Dr. Albert Hofmann, the discoverer of LSD, is an outstanding overview of human use of plant hallucinogens throughout history and around the world.

Photographic Books

There are many high-quality photographic books of jungles, including the magnificent *Rainforests of the World,* by Art Wolfe and Ghillean Prance; *The Rainforests: A Celebration,* edited by Lisa Silcock; *Beneath the Canopy—Wildlife of the Latin American Rain Forest,* by Downs

Matthews and Kevin Schafer; and the stunning *Jewels of the Rainforest—Poison Frogs of the Family Dendrobatidae,* by Jerry G. Walls.

Also recommended: *Rain Forests and Cloud Forests,* with text by Michael Emsley and striking photographs by Kjell B. Sandved. Loren McIntyre, the celebrated photographer whose work graced the pages of *National Geographic* for years, produced two luscious books of images: *Amazonia,* a Sierra Club Book, and *Exploring South America,* published by Potter. These out-of-print books are usually available from Alibris (*www.alibris.com*) or on interlibrary loan.

Travel Books

For general travel information I highly recommend books published by the NTC/Contemporary Publishing Group. Their now-legendary *South American Handbook* has been the gold standard for decades. The series currently includes the following titles for countries with significant regions of tropical lowlands:

- *South American Handbook*
- *Mexico and Central American Handbook*
- *Caribbean Islands Handbook*
- *India Handbook*
- *Laos Handbook*
- *Cambodia Handbook*
- *Vietnam Handbook*
- *Thailand Handbook*

Weather Information

My first research project in the tropical lowlands took place on the Cayapa River in northwestern Ecuador, near the Colombian border. A young medical student, I arrived on the river just after Christmas—the beginning of the wet season. A local missionary, Rev. Lester Meisenheimer, commented, "I don't know how much you will get done this time of year. The rainy season, you know."

"What's a little rain," I thought. A "little" rain is no big deal—but how about 435 inches of rain? To put that deluge in perspective, consider this: the midwestern and the Appalachian states get about 40 inches of rain in a good year. With 435 inches, the low-lying clouds empty a daily torrent of water that varies from a truly deafening roar that shakes the earth beneath your feet to a constant drizzle—day and night—that saturates everything you own.

Trips into the rainforest should be scheduled for the dry season whenever possible, because trails are more serviceable for trekking at that time. Group travel is especially unwise during the height of the rainy season due to the frustration of constantly sliding around on muddy trails, the increased risk of crossing wet log bridges, and the demoralizing effects of the constant dampness and gloomy, overcast skies. Such conditions are guaranteed to bring out the worst in participants.

Information on weather patterns may be obtained from agencies of national governments, anthropologists, missionaries, and often from standard travel guides. The excellent series *World Survey of Climatology*, edited by Werner Schwerdtfeger, is exceptionally helpful in getting an historical sense of climate patterns, even in fairly remote tropical regions. Region-specific volumes from this series are usually available in large reference libraries or can be procured through interlibrary loan.

Recommended Books to Take into the Jungle

In addition to this book, take *Field Guide to Wilderness Medicine*, by Paul Auerbach, Howard Donner, and Eric Weiss. Three experts share their vast experience-based knowledge. For injuries and other emergencies in the wilderness setting, this portable book is simply unrivaled. Also consider *A Comprehensive Guide to Wilderness and Travel Medicine*, by Eric Weiss. This handbook is strong on improvisation in the wilderness and should be considered if you wish to carry something that is even more compact than the *Field Guide to Wilderness Medicine*.

If you plan to travel with a child, include in your pack Dr. Barbara Kennedy's pocked-sized *Caring for Children in the Outdoors*.

2

MEDICAL PREPARATIONS

Health and Safety Information
  Prior to Travel
Locating Physicians for
  Predeparture and
  Posttrip Consultation
Travelers' Medical Insurance and
  Emergency Medical
  Transport
Immunizations
Medical Kit

When someone comes to my travel clinic for pretravel advice, I always spend a few minutes familiarizing myself with the individual's planned itinerary, current health status, past history of significant health problems, and, especially, their history of immunizations. Also, I ask if there have been any reactions to drugs or insect stings, and I obtain a complete listing of current medications the patient is taking.

These questions, coupled with a limited physical examination, allow me to assess the individual's fitness—physically and psychologically—for their particular travel agenda and individualize a plan of prevention and health maintenance. Often patients are going to areas of the world where health standards are equal to or even superior to those encountered in most regions of the United States. For such individuals my advice is simple: "Take twice the amount of money you *think* you need, and half the amount of clothes."

In our college town, however, there are hordes of adventure-minded students who want to see the world—a good thing—but insist on "going native." In practical terms, this means they plan to wander around barefoot and eat what the locals eat. What they fail to appreciate is this: in many desperately poor nations, the people they encounter are the hearty, immune souls who meet all the criteria for the "survival-of-the-fittest" school of natural selection. Our relatively tender students, alas, are sitting ducks for every imaginable infectious microbe. Such individuals need to understand the need for wearing shoes (to prevent the intrusion of parasites such as hookworm and strongyloides) and to avoid certain foods and drink (to lessen the likelihood of travelers' diarrhea due to *E. Coli* or giardia).

HEALTH AND SAFETY INFORMATION PRIOR TO TRAVEL

Today, excellent health information for the traveler going to tropical rainforest regions is available in books, by telephone hot lines, and on the Internet. In this section I have named several sources of reliable information. To keep it simple, however, the reader can log onto a single web site—**www.cdc.gov**—to access all the information required for informed travel decision-making short of a consultation with a physician who specializes in travel medicine (something I recommend as well).

www.cdc.gov

This is the mother lode of health information for all international travel. Logging on this single site allows the user to promptly access up-to-date health information on travel to specific regions. It also includes essential links such as the U.S. State Department's Travelers' Advisory Hotline.

I strongly recommend that all travelers, novice and seasoned, start at the Centers for Disease Control (CDC) site and familiarize themselves with the current recommendations. Remember, expert consensus recommendations on health information and travel safety can change rapidly—all the more reason to get the most up-to-date information possible!

International Travelers' Hot Line: Centers for Disease Control and Prevention

The CDC's telephone hot line, **877-FYI-TRIP**, provides up-to-date, authoritative voice recordings on diseases specific to international travel and instructions on how to order printed material, such as *Health Information for International Travel*.

Travelers' Advisory: U.S. State Department

If you're traveling to an area of *political unrest* (usually a euphemism for bomb threats, hijackings, and hostage-taking), the U.S. State Department's Travelers' Advisory Hotline has updated information on terrorist threats and political uprisings, often regionalized by province or state within a country. Phone: 202–647–5225.

Consular Information Sheets are available for every country of the world and include such information as the location of the U.S. Embassy or Consulate in the subject country, unusual immigration practices, health conditions, minor political disturbances, unusual currency and entry regulations, crime and security information, and drug penalties.

Travel Warnings and Consular Information sheets can be accessed via the Bureau of Consular Affairs home page: *www.travel. state.gov.* This site has numerous useful links.

LOCATING PHYSICIANS FOR PREDEPARTURE AND POSTTRIP CONSULTATION

In recent years travel clinics have sprung up across North America and Europe for those whose itinerary puts them at risk, particularly from diseases carried by insects or from water-borne infections in countries where health standards are lax. These clinics are especially suited for those individuals with preexisting health problems. Travel clinics are staffed by physicians who have a professional interest in the emerging specialty of travel medicine and who often have had special training in tropical diseases. Usually, though not always, travel clinics are associated with a medical school or university hospital. The following resources will prove helpful in locating physicians who can provide in-depth predeparture consultation services.

Clinical Consultants Directory

The American Society of Tropical Medicine and Hygiene (ASTMH), the principal organization in the United States representing scientists, clinicians, and others with interests in the prevention and control of tropical diseases, publishes a useful Clinical Consultants Directory. This booklet contains a list of physicians who offer clinical consultative service in tropical medicine, medical parasitology, and travelers' health. (The list does not imply endorsement, verification of credentials, or expertise of those listed.) For further information contact the American Society of Tropical Medicine and Hygiene, 60 Revere Drive, Suite 500, Northbrook, IL 60062, USA. Tel: 847–480–9592. Fax: 847–480–9282. E-mail: *astmh@astmh.org.* An electronic version of the directory is located at the ASTMH web site at *www.astmh.org* and is updated several times each year.

ISTM Clinic Directory

The International Society of Travel Medicine (ISTM), dedicated to the advancement of the specialty of travel medicine and the promotion of healthy and safe travel, boasts 1,200 members in 53 countries. The ISTM Clinic Directory, with travel clinics listed by location, may be accessed on the society's web site: *www.istm.org.* Address and contact information: International Society of Travel Medicine, P.O. Box 871089, Stone Mountain GA, 30087–0028, USA. Phone: 770–736–7060.

Travel Medicine

Travel Medicine (www.travmed.com) offers an extensive listing of travel medicine specialists who can provide health advice you may need prior to departure.

Posttrip Physician Consultation

Upon returning from a trip to jungle regions, a consultation with a travel medicine specialist is in order if there has been a change in your pretrip health status, especially if you have any of these symptoms:

- Fever
- Diarrhea (or constipation)
- Abdominal pain
- Chronic cough
- Skin rash
- Weight loss
- Fatigue

Locating Physicians and Hospitals in a Foreign Country

Both ISTM (see above) and the International Association for Medical Assistance to Travelers (IAMAT) are good resources for locating physicians and hospitals in a foreign country. IAMAT is a nonprofit information and physician-patient networking organization of 1,200 physicians around the world providing politically unfiltered information on disease risk in specific countries. IAMAT publishes a booklet that lists English-speaking physicians and health clinics worldwide where competent medical care is available to the traveler.

To contact IAMAT in the United States, phone 716–754–4883; in Canada, 519–836–0102.

The U.S. Department of State (*http://travel.state.gov/medical.html*) offers this advice: "If an American citizen becomes seriously ill or injured abroad, a U.S. consular officer can assist in locating appropriate medical services and informing family or friends. If necessary, a consular officer can also assist in transfer of funds from the United States. However, payment of hospital and other expenses is the responsibility of the traveler."

TRAVELERS' MEDICAL INSURANCE AND EMERGENCY MEDICAL TRANSPORT

Travelers should check with their existing health insurance carrier to determine if medical care is covered abroad. Also, be sure to check with your insurance company or HMO to see if you need preauthorization *before* you travel overseas.

A number of insurance companies provide policies that pay for medical care overseas and provide medical assistance to travelers. One such company, International SOS Assistance, Inc. (*www.intsos.com*), provides a broad range of services, including 24-hour medical assistance, emergency medication, emergency evacuation, and an optional policy that covers hospital and physician costs. Another popular company, Access America (*www.etravelprotection.com*), offers an array of products, including emergency medical coverage and emergency medical transportation benefits. American Express (*travel.americanexpress. com*) offers coverage for unexpected medical or dental emergencies and evacuation/medical transportation. American Express Platinum (800–345–2639) cardholders are entitled to emergency medical transport.

The U.S. State Department (*http://travel.state.gov/medical.html*) provides an extensive list of air ambulance/med-evac companies as well as travel insurance companies.

IMMUNIZATIONS

Standard Immunizations

Tetanus-Diphtheria A booster should be administered once every 10 years for life.

Hepatitis A All travelers going to countries with substandard sanitation should receive hepatitis A vaccine. There are two hepatitis A vaccines currently available in the United States, Havrix and

VAQTA. Both vaccines provide a high degree of protection within 2 weeks. A booster is required between 6 and 12 months after initial vaccination. Following the complete two-dose series, protection may persist for as long as 20 years.

Persons traveling to high-risk areas less than 2 weeks after the initial dose of hepatitis A vaccine should also be given pooled immune globulin (IG) at a different injection site than the hepatitis A vaccine.

Hepatitis B The prevalence of hepatitis B carriers in populations inhabiting jungle regions of the world is often very high. The risk of travelers acquiring hepatitis B is increased by the prevalence of hepatitis B carriers in the local population, the extent of direct contact with blood, secretions or intimate sexual contact with infected persons, and the duration of travel.

In the past, most experts recommended restricted use of hepatitis B vaccine for long-term (greater than a 6-month stay) travelers going to high-prevalence areas, and any short-term travelers who may have contact with blood or body fluids (e.g., health care workers). At present, hepatitis B vaccination can be recommended as part of a standard immunization program regardless of travel.

Two vaccines, Recombivax HB and Engerix-B, are available in the United States. Either requires a three-dose series with the second dose given 1 month after the first dose, and the third dose given 6 months after the first dose. Vaccination ideally should begin 6 months before travel.

Measles Measles vaccination is not necessary for persons with documented physician-diagnosed measles or laboratory (serologic) evidence of measles immunity. The vaccine should be administered to persons born after 1956 who have not received a prior booster dose.

Typhoid Travelers to tropical regions should receive typhoid vaccine. Of the three typhoid vaccines currently available for use in the United States, only two can be recommended: Vivotif Berna or Typhim Vi. Vivotif Berna is an oral vaccine. A new injectable vaccine, Typhim Vi, has essentially replaced the older injectable Typhoid USP vaccine. The older vaccine frequently causes unwanted side effects including fever, headache, and severe local pain or swelling at the injection site.

The oral typhoid vaccine should be boosted every 5 years; the injectable Typhim Vi, every 2 years.

Special Immunizations

Yellow Fever There are two yellow fever endemic zones: Sub-Saharan Africa and tropical regions of South America. Travelers to the province of Darien in Panama should also consider vaccination against yellow fever. *Health Information for International Travel* lists yellow fever requirements by country. The International Travelers' Hot Line at CDC (877–FYI–TRIP, web site *www.cdc.gov/travel*) also gives up-to-date information on countries with current yellow fever risk. A booster dose is given every 10 years.

Rabies Rabid animals, particularly dogs, are encountered in Central and South America, Africa, and Asia. Vampire bats, fruit bats, and insectivorous bats all can transmit rabies; these bats are found throughout Mexico, Central and South America. Travelers, particularly trekkers in jungle regions of the Americas, should consider preexposure human diploid cell rabies vaccine (HDCV).

Polio Immunized travelers who plan to travel outside the Western Hemisphere should receive a one-time booster dose of injectable polio vaccine (e-IPV).

Japanese Encephalitis Japanese encephalitis is a mosquitoborne viral encephalitis encountered in certain rural areas of Southeast Asia, the Indian subcontinent, and the Philippines. Travelers should consider immunization if they expect to spend more than 30 days in areas where unprotected outdoor evening and nighttime exposure to mosquitoes is anticipated.

Meningococcal Meningitis Travelers to the meningitis-belt region of sub-Saharan Africa during the months of December to June should consider receiving vaccination.

Cholera The risk of cholera in travelers is very low and no cholera vaccination requirements exist for entry or exit in any country. The CDC does not recommend cholera vaccine for travelers.

Plague The risk to travelers is small and vaccination is rarely indicated. Individuals such as field biologists or those who work in areas with active epidemics and will have significant exposure to rodents and fleas might consider this vaccine.

Influenza Vaccine Persons traveling into remote regions of Amazonia where Indian groups live in isolation should receive yearly influenza vaccinations to reduce the likelihood of inadvertently transmitting disease to these high-risk native inhabitants. Influenza in Amerindian populations can have especially lethal consequences.

Other Preventive Measures

Travelers' Diarrhea and Malaria Travelers' diarrhea is a common problem for visitors to third-world countries. Preventive strategies are discussed on pages 127–28.

Malaria is a potentially deadly parasitic illness and is encountered in virtually all jungle regions of the world. For an expanded discussion of preventive measures, turn to page 132.

MEDICAL KIT

A physician member of a research team in Brazil was stung in the mouth when he accidentally ingested a wasplike insect while drinking from a soft drink can. Within minutes, he began to itch, first around his nose and facial area, then his entire body. As he frantically scratched at his skin, hives erupted on his arms, and his lips suddenly began to swell. "I'm having an anaphylactic reaction!" he cried. "Get the EpiPen—quick!"

As the expedition leader tore open the medical kit, the victim's breathing began to deteriorate. "Hurry," he moaned. Seconds after the EpiPen Auto-Injector was located, the gray safety cap was popped off and the business end of the device jammed against the victim's thigh. The spring-loaded auto-injector instantly shot 0.3 cc of life-saving epinephrine into his system. Minutes later, he was feeling better. After a second blast of epinephrine and a dose of Benadryl by mouth, he made a full recovery.

Having the right medications and equipment, especially for emergencies, is essential for travel in isolated regions of rainforest. It is critical that all team members know where to locate medications and equipment. High-quality, neatly organized, rugged, prepackaged wilderness medical kits are available from a number of suppliers, including Chinook Medical Gear, Inc. (*www.chinookmed.com*) and Travel Medicine, Inc. (*www.travmed.com*). Both Chinook and Travel Medicine can prepare customized kits.

The basic personal medical kit and the expedition kits discussed below are suitable for jungle travel.

A caveat: the Wilderness Medical Society advises that it is inappropriate to pack medications and equipment when no team member has the knowledge or experience to use them safely.

Personal Medical Kit

The recommended purchase is a sturdy organizer bag with clear vinyl compartments for the personal medical kit. For extra protection, seal pills and capsules in resealable plastic bags to avoid moisture absorption from the humid tropical environment.

Here's what you need:

1. ACE wrap. Two 3" or 4" ACE wraps should be carried for snakebite management. (See snake on page 112.) One wrap

will be used as a constricting band to limit venom spread. (For truly ultra-light packing, use a length of 1" penrose drain instead of ACE wrap to use as a constricting band.) The other will be used to secure a SAM splint (or a stick) for immobilization to the envenomated limb. While these popular wraps have limited, if any, use for stabilizing joint injuries, they serve to provide compression.

2. Pepto-Bismol in tablet form is an effective over-the-counter preparation for preventing and treating common travelers' diarrhea. It also is useful for heartburn and indigestion. Pepto-Bismol tends to turn the tongue and stool black.

3. Benadryl is safe and effective as an antihistamine, for motion sickness, and as a nighttime sleep aid.

4. Ciprofloxin hydrochloride 500 mg tablets (Cipro). Cipro is highly active against the important bacterial causes of enteritis, including *Escherichia coli, Vibrio cholerae, Salmonella, Shigella, Campylobacter jejuni, Aeromonas,* and *Yersinia enterocolitica.* Cipro can also be used for acute sinusitis, urinary tract infections, skin infections, and lower respiratory infections. Prescription required.

5. Clotrimazole and betamethasone dipropionate cream (Lotrisone). Lotrisone has the dual advantage of having antifungal properties and a sufficiently potent steroid for steroid-sensitive rashes. Prescription required for this combination drug.

6. Epinephrine auto-injector (EpiPen/EpiPen Jr. Auto-Injector). For emergency treatment of severe allergic reactions to insect stings, foods, or drugs, EpiPen/EpiPen Jr. provides a virtually foolproof delivery system for speeding a single dose of epinephrine into the victim's bloodstream. Prescription required.

7. Ibuprofen 600 mg tablets. Ibuprofen is a good choice for mild to moderate pain from such problems as menstrual cramps, rheumatoid arthritis, and osteoarthritis. It also lowers elevated body temperature caused by common infectious diseases. Prescription required for the 600 mg size. Ibuprofen 200 mg is available without prescription.

8. Ketorolac (Toradol) 60 mg for injection. Toradol provides good short-term relief for moderate to severe pain. It is preferred over narcotics only because it is less likely to cause

problems with customs officials and police. Prescription required.

9. Lidocaine hydrochloride. This local anesthetic agent may be required for relief of the excruciating pain resulting from stingray envenomation or conga ant or caterpillar stings. It should be infiltrated around the wound area. Carry a dental aspirating syringe, 25 GA long needles, and lidocaine in carpules used by dentists. The carpules are protected, easy to carry, and more user-friendly in the rainforest setting. Prescription required.

10. Metronidazole 250 mg tablets. Metronidazole is excellent for treating giardiasis, acute amebic dysentery, or *Trichomonas* vaginitis. Prescription required.

11. Mupirocin ointment 2 percent (Bactroban). This exceptionally effective ointment should be immediately applied to burns, abrasions, lacerations, and ruptured blisters, which can rapidly become infected in the tropics. Male trekkers report Bactroban aids in reducing the inflammation where the skin of the scrotal sac or cloth from soggy underpants rubs against the thighs. Prescription required.

12. Permethrin 5 percent cream (Elimite) and 1 percent shampoo (Nix). Many natives, especially in the tropics of Central and South America, are infested with scabies and head lice. Travelers who have been in close contact with heavily infested tribal peoples or shared clothing or head gear with them should apply permethrin cream and shampoo before returning home. In the United States, Elimite is a prescription drug; Nix is sold over the counter.

13. SAM Splint, full length and finger sizes. This remarkable splint is lightweight, waterproof, reusable, and not affected by temperature extremes. With a thousand and one uses, the SAM Splint is sold in sporting stores and is available from suppliers of medical gear specifically oriented to the outdoors, such as Chinook Medical Gear, Inc. (*www.chinookmed.com*).

14. Sulfacetamide sodium ophthalmic solution 10 percent (Sodium Sulamyd). This product is excellent for treating conjunctivitis, corneal ulcers, or other superficial ocular infections.

(Some eye specialists prefer one of the newer ophthalmic solutions such as Ciloxan.) Prescription required.

15. Sunscreen. Sunscreen is essential in open areas such as rivers or jungle clearings. Sunscreens designated "waterproof" retain their full sun protection factor rating for longer periods during sweating or water immersion than do products designated "water resistant." Opaque formulations are excellent for the nose, lips, and ears. Visitors to the tropics should wear lightweight, long-sleeved shirts and a wide-brimmed hat when exposed to the sun for prolonged periods. Available in any drugstore or sporting store.

16. Tramadol hydrochloride tablets 50 mg (Ultram). For moderate to severe pain. Prescription required.

17. Antimalarial medication, which is discussed in Chapter 11.

18. Oral rehydration mix and medication for travelers' diarrhea, which is discussed in Chapter 11.

Common sense dictates supplementary items. Women on long trips should add miconazole vaginal suppositories to treat yeast infections (an alternative is Diflucan, one 150 mg tablet taken as a single oral dose); older men might take a 16 Fr Foley catheter and sterile lubricating jelly for dealing with problems arising from prostatic hypertrophy. Albuterol metered dose inhalers should be included for known asthmatics or anyone with a history of exercise-induced bronchoconstriction.

Trauma Checklist for High-Risk Expeditions

The following items should be considered for high-risk outings where major trauma may occur at some distance from definitive medical care. Use of these devices requires special medical training.

1. Airway supplies
    Endotracheal tubes
    Cricothyrotomy cannula or catheter

2. Chest tube set

3. Blood pressure cuff

4. Stethoscope

5. Trauma/Suture/Surgical Kit

Dental Kit

I also recommend the following for inclusion in a wilderness dental kit:

- Mouth mirror
- Dental floss
- Cavit no-mix temporary filling material
- Eugenol (oil of cloves) topical analgesic
- IRM powder for recementing crowns
- Dental aspirating syringe, 25 GA long needles and lidocaine (or marcaine) in carpules used by dentists

Prepackaged dental emergency kits are also available.

3

GEAR

Footwear
Clothing
Bedding
Backpacks
Other Useful Items
Photography

Gear must hold up under difficult jungle travel conditions that include heat, wetness, and mud. At this writing there is no line of advertised gear ideally suited for the traveler who plans to spend time off the beaten path in the tropics. In the United States, L.L. Bean, Inc. (*www.llbean.com*) and Recreational Equipment, Inc. (REI) (*www.rei.com*) are good sources for reasonably priced and reliable equipment, that, while not always ideal for the tropics, are usually satisfactory.

The idea is to *travel as light as possible*. The more stuff that is packed, the greater the likelihood of breakdowns, complications, and misery. Equipment freaks who go in for lots of unnecessarily expensive, colorful gear will be disappointed by the following discussion of basic equipment. These items have, however, withstood the test of time over years of long-distance tropical trekking.

FOOTWEAR

Since feet absorb more punishment than any other part of the body, good footwear is the single most important item of gear. This is the one place where a person absolutely must not carry inferior equipment. If the feet cannot go, nothing can go.

Military-style "jungle boots" are unsuitable for serious, long-distance trekking. After an hour of hard walking through streams and muddy trails, blisters will form on every surface of the foot and the skin will peel off in sheets, bringing a jungle trip to a premature end. Furthermore, safely crossing log bridges and mossy, slime-covered river rocks is almost impossible in these boots.

I thought nothing could be worse than military issue boots until a participant on a Brazilian expedition showed up wearing expensive, custom-made, knee-high leather boots. In less than 30 minutes on the trail, his heels and soles were bloody and raw. Leather snake-proof boots give the wearer a somewhat dashing appearance and may be okay for the rattlesnake-infested scrub lands of Florida and Alabama, but they have no place on a jungle expedition.

Two pairs of shoes are needed: one suitable for the wet, slippery conditions imposed by the trail, and another that meets the need for dryness and comfort in camp.

Trail Shoes

The following features are desirable in trail shoes:

1. Uppers that hit just above or just below the ankles. Some people choose the above-ankle design, reasoning that the extra height gives some added snake protection.

2. Extra protection over the big toe. Protective rubber or leather toecaps help keep the big toe from being severely battered and bruised.

3. Moderately deep-tread outsoles. Traction on rugged and muddy terrain is important. Running shoes with hard, "high-impact" soles should not be worn because they become slippery on wet logs or river rocks.

4. Quick drying time. Uppers of Cordura nylon and split leather, in addition to resisting abrasion and being somewhat breathable, dry out surprisingly fast when placed in the sun. Even though hiking shoes usually become soaked within minutes on the trail, it is a psychologic boost to start off each new day with dry (or less than soggy!) shoes. Since jungle travelers can be in waist-high water many times each day while on the trail, waterproof shoes with Gore-Tex liners are not essential.

5. Snagproof design. Shoes or boots with "quick-lace" steel hooks should be avoided: vines and weeds become tangled around the metal hooks, causing the wearer to stumble and

pulling the laces untied. Shoelaces should always be double knotted.

6. Lightweight.

7. Well broken in.

Any good brand with the above mentioned characteristics will suffice. Over the years, I've used Nike, Merrell, Hi-Tec, and Vasquez footwear; they all seem to do the job.

Camp Boots

Footwear needs are very different in camp. Being wet on the trail is one thing, but the trekker wants dry feet in camp. Here are the key features:

1. A boot. Shoes, although excellent for the trail, do not work out well in camp. A boot that comes to midcalf keeps mud off the feet and pants.

2. Rubber construction. Rubber remains an excellent material for keeping water away from the feet.

3. Rubber lug soles for traction. When rubber-soled boots are worn, however, extreme caution is needed when crossing log bridges (even dry ones) and walking on slippery moss or slime-covered rocks by the river's edge.

4. Lightweight. On the trail, camp boots must be carried in a pack, so the lighter the better.

Discount stores such as Wal-Mart usually carry lightweight, lug-soled rubber boots that meet the criteria for jungle camp boots.

Other Options

The lightweight, comfortable, mesh/neoprene fabric "water" shoes that have become popular in recent years for beach and sailboarding activities may have a place on river trips in which substantial time will be spent in dugout canoes or rubber rafts.

Thongs and open-toe sandals are fine for most towns and cities in the tropics, but in certain jungle regions such as the Amazon Basin, exposed feet invite hordes of biting insects.

The jungle traveler must never go barefoot. Plant spines and glass can puncture the feet, and larvae of ubiquitous parasites such as hookworm and strongyloidiasis can enter through the skin. The burrowing jigger flea, *Tunga penetrans,* is a serious pest and can be avoided by wearing shoes.

Socks

Cotton or thin synthetic socks should be worn in the jungle to decrease the risk of blisters from wet trail shoes, to reduce insect bites (particularly from no-see-ums), and to lessen the risk of cuts from sawgrass.

CLOTHING

In many countries military green or camouflage-style clothing is completely out of the question. This is particularly true in military dictatorships or in remote border regions. To be mistaken for a guerrilla or foreign infiltrator by the military, police, or security (undercover) forces can lead to harassment, detention, or worse.

Hats

For protection from radiant heat and things that tend to land on a person's head in the forest, the traveler should wear a lightweight, light-colored hat that has a medium or wide brim. It need not be waterproof, but it should be made of material that can be wadded up. A useful feature is a fastener on each side to snap the brim up for traveling on the trail. A pith helmet, widely regarded as a silly affectation, is fine for open savanna and river trips, but on the trail, branches would knock it off a person's head every few minutes.

Pullover

A drenching rain may leave a person feeling chilled and uncomfortable, particularly when traveling mainly by canoe or raft. (Chilling generally is not a problem when hiking on the trail so long as the person keeps moving.) A Dacron polyester fleece pullover such as L.L. Bean's Polarlite Pullover, REI's Polarlite Sweater, or one of the excellent pullovers made by Patagonia will keep a person warm. When these garments get wet, they should be wrung out so that they continue to offer thermal protection. Professional white-water boatmen working in tropical regions generally pack a polyester outerwear garment.

Shirts

Two light-colored, ultra-lightweight, long-sleeved cotton shirts should be taken. One of these shirts will be the trail shirt. At the end of the day, it should be washed and rinsed so that it will be ready, although perhaps still damp, the next morning. The second shirt can be used in camp or as a spare for the trail. Do not be enticed into buying synthetic shirts guaranteed to wick away moisture; these expensive shirts are fine for saltwater fly-fishing but, despite advertising to the contrary, they assure instant misery as jungle trail shirts. They will leave you sweaty, sticky, and stinky.

In camp, if there are not many no-see-ums and mosquitoes, a lightweight, short-sleeved cotton shirt comes in handy. Two should be packed. A four-pocket style called the *guayabera*, favored by men throughout Latin America and the Caribbean, is ideal. La Casa de Las Guayaberas, Naroca Plaza, 5840 S.W. 8th Street, Miami, FL 33144 (305–266–9683; fax 305–267–1687) has an exceptional selection of short- and long-sleeved guayaberas; be sure to specify 100 percent cotton.

Pants

Two pairs of ultra-lightweight, light-colored cotton pants are needed. One pair is worn on the trail during the entire trip. Trail pants should be washed often. The other pair is worn around camp and in towns along the way. Jeans become waterlogged as soon as they become wet and are totally unsuitable for tropical trekking. Although synthetic *shirts* are unsuitable, Nylon Supplex® *pants* can substitute for cotton on the trail. Pants sold by Sportif (800–776–7843) hold up well, are quick drying, have a built-in mesh brief, and meet criteria for comfort on the trail. Pants with zip-off legs to create instant shorts don't hold up well on the trail and should be avoided.

Belt

Nylon, double O-ring style adjustable belts are suitable for jungle conditions. Stay away from leather belts; they collect green mold almost overnight.

Undergarments

Underpants should be made of cotton. Bras should be mostly cotton; female trekkers report that sports bras are decidedly preferable to traditional styles.

Poncho

An ultra-thin waterproof poncho is useful on rafting or canoe trips and in villages but is worthless on the trail.

BEDDING

Flannel Sheet

First-time visitors to tropical rainforests are surprised to discover how uncomfortably cold it gets between midnight and sunrise. A cotton sheet does not provide enough warmth, a blanket is too heavy, and a summer-weight sleeping bag retains too much body heat. A flannel sheet, sewn together like a mummy bag (40 × 90 inches), but without a taper, provides suitable warmth either in a hammock or on a pad.

Foot Warmers

Many inhabitants of the tropical forests sleep with their feet near a fire that is tended throughout the night. They have learned that the chill of damp, cool jungle nights can be lessened as long as the feet stay warm. Using disposable "Grabber Toe Heaters" (available from REI *www.rei.com*) wrapped within a sock accomplishes essentially the same thing. These inexpensive air-activated disposable packets are made with environmentally safe, nontoxic materials and keep the feet warm for up to 6 hours.

Hammock

Soft, cloth hammocks are exquisitely comfortable and lovely to look at, but they are too bulky and too heavy for trips. After a few days they begin to smell. Fishnet cotton hammocks are comfortable and lightweight but tend to fall apart within hours or days. The so-called camping tent-hammocks or military tent-hammocks seem adequate, but they are usually bulky, heavy, impossible to sling properly, extremely uncomfortable, hot, unstable, and *never* able to keep the rain out in a heavy tropical downpour.

The nylon "Double Hammock," available in Wal-Mart stores, has proved nearly ideal for jungle travel. (Model EZ-190 made by E-Z Sales Manufacturing, 1432 West 166 St., Gardena, CA 90247.) It is compact, lightweight, durable, and reasonably comfortable. It cannot rot or absorb odors. For easier handling, the ski rope tie-end lines that are sold with the "Double Hammock" should be replaced with ⅜-inch double-braided nylon rope.

Therm-a-Rest

The Therm-a-Rest foam pad is the choice of expedition organizers throughout the world. It combines the insulating qualities of foam and the cushioning of an air mattress, rolls up to a compact size, and inflates on its own when the valve is opened. The Therm-a-Rest stuff sack is excellent for transporting the pad.

The traveler who will be sleeping on a pad should pack a good-quality 1½- × 2½-yard plastic ground sheet. The ground sheet should not be placed directly on the jungle floor, where stinging insects and snakes abound. It should be used only in a hut or on an elevated platform. The ground sheet may also come in handy for temporary rain protection and for keeping bow spray off a person or gear during water travel.

Mosquito Netting

A mosquito net designed for use with a hammock is basically a rectangular box that is open at the bottom with sleeves at each end panel for the passage of the ropes by which the hammock is slung. Such nets are hard to find outside the tropics. Fortunately, a serviceable mosquito net can easily be made from "no-see-um netting," which, though not a regular catalog item, is available by request from REI. (See pg. 93).

BACKPACKS

A sturdy, well-designed backpack should be used to carry gear. 3M Scotchlite™ Reflective Material should be sewn onto the back of each backpack. Iron Horse Safety Specialists (800–323–5889, fax 214–340–7775, e-mail *ihss1@aol.com*) sells red-orange reflective material, product #8986, for daytime visibility, and reflective silver, product #8930, for nighttime reflectivity.

On serious jungle treks, porters carry most of the gear. This frees expedition members to carry much lighter loads.

Backpack for Porter

An internal-frame backpack of 3,000- to 4,000-cubic inch capacity is a good size. It should have external pockets for quick access to liter-sized water bottles.

Indigenous peoples the world over are accustomed to carrying packs and hauling loads with a strap known as a tumpline slung over the forehead or chest. Many natives, including Amazonian Indians, dislike using the shoulder straps that come as standard equipment on backpacks. Given enough straps, almost any native porter can quickly rig a satisfactory tumpline on a backpack. Don't offer any suggestions on how to rig the tumpline; you'll just confuse the issue. If you are traveling in South America with jungle-dwelling Indians and you don't have extra straps, not to worry. These natives will strip bark from saplings and, in minutes, fashion an adequate tumpline.

Personal Pack

A daypack of 1,200- to 2,000-cubic inch capacity is useful for carrying a camera, snack food, and other gear that must be kept handy. A built-in waterproof liner will keep perspiration from wicking into the bag and wetting everything inside. The pack should have two outside pockets for quick access to liter-sized water bottles.

Pack for River Trips

A durable, waterproof "dry" bag, used by river runners, is worth considering, especially if the trip will involve spending days or weeks at a time in dugout canoes or rubber rafts. Most of these packs, however, cannot stand up to the demands of long-distance overland trekking. The straps tend to be uncomfortable and frequently rip out on the trail.

OTHER USEFUL ITEMS

The following items are available from a variety of sources, including discount stores and camping suppliers such as REI.

Antifogging Solution for Eyeglasses

Antifog solution, available from dive shops, reduces humidity-induced fogging of glasses.

Batteries

Alkaline batteries should be brought from home. Batteries sold in third-world nations do not last long and often leak.

Binoculars

The traveler who is an avid birdwatcher or enjoys watching butterflies or seeking out orchids high on distant limbs will want to pack a pair of binoculars that is lightweight, compact, shockproof, and waterproof or water resistant.

Camp Soap

A biodegradable soap should be used. The soap Campsuds works in hot, cold, fresh, or salt water and cleans just about anything: dishes, clothing, hair, and skin.

Candles

Electricity tends to fail at unpredictable times in small towns and even in cities in third-world countries. Travelers should carry dripless candles. Spring-loaded candle lanterns should be avoided; they give off an anemic glow, gum up, get crushed or broken, and basically waste space in the pack.

Cleats

Covell "Ice Walker Quick Clip Cleats" (available from REI) can be instantly snapped on prior to crossing intimidating log bridges and promptly snapped off at the other end.

Cup and Plate

A large Lexan polycarbonate cup is unbreakable, does not retain taste or odor, and serves the role of cup, bowl, and plate. Travelers who feel the need for an actual plate should buy one made of indestructible Melamine.

Ear Plugs

Travel in the tropics often involves flying in incredibly loud helicopters, cargo planes, or short take-off and landing (STOL) aircraft. Sponge ear plugs that roll up and fit in the ear canal offer inexpensive, effective protection against hearing damage. Low pressure foam ear plugs, manufactured by Howard Leight Industries (*www.howardleight.com*), are very comfortable and easily inserted.

Fishing Supplies

For additional "food insurance" when traveling in remote, uninhabited regions, the jungle traveler should carry 75 feet of 20-pound-test fishing line, two 12-inch steel leaders with swivels, and a few hooks. Breakdown travel rods and spincast reels should be considered for sport fishing or adding fresh meat to the daily provisions.

Throughout the tropics most species of fish find Rat-L-Trap lures, particularly the chrome and blue combination, irresistible.

Garbage Bags

Four 30-gallon capacity and four 13-gallon capacity plastic garbage bags come in handy for holding clothes, bedding, and other items that must stay absolutely dry, as well as for keeping dirty boots isolated from clean items in the backpack.

GPS

Global positioning system (GPS) units are lightweight (as little as 5 oz.), compact, and display precise latitude, longitude, and altitude—day or night, rain or shine. With a GPS unit and a topo map or satellite image (with coordinates), you always know exactly where you are. The price of these instruments has dropped to a level anyone can afford. The Garmin eTrex Summit is a combination GPS, altimeter, and electronic compass. When traveling in minimally explored regions, serious trekkers and expedition leaders should pack a GPS unit.

Expedition organizers who plan to lead large groups into minimally explored, high-risk regions should consider carrying the GyPSI™ 406 Personal Locator Beacon (ACR Electronics, *www.acrelectronics.com*), which transmits on 406 MHZ with a digitally coded distress signal and has a waterproof GPS and programming interface to transmit GPS data for even faster response in an emergency. (See Chapter 15.)

Headlamp

Battery-operated headlamps offer hands-free convenience and are perfect for reading at night in the hammock. Choose a cordless headlamp that is lightweight, durable, and shines at least 10 hours on a set of batteries.

For emergency use or for making a stumble-free, late-night dash to the latrine, the miniature Photon Microlight II is a good choice. This powerful light fits on a zipper pull or can be conveniently hung around your neck.

Inflatable Cushion or Pillow

If a lot of time will be spent sitting in a dugout canoe or aluminum boat, a small, durable, cloth-covered inflatable cushion is recommended.

Insect Repellent

To repel mosquitoes, flies, ticks, chiggers, fleas, and gnats (but not no-see-ums), buy any spray insect repellent containing 15 to 30 percent DEET. Avoid formulations containing higher than 30 percent DEET, often called "jungle juice": they may pose health hazards. Longer-acting and potentially safer formulations such as DEET incorporated into liposomes (LIPODEET) are undergoing evaluation trials.

Technique is critical when applying insect repellent containing DEET. Before dressing, the person should spray the ankles, lower legs, and waist. After the socks are put on, a band should be sprayed around the top; a band should also be sprayed around both pant legs to midcalf. A light spray to the shirt, front and back, may also help. The hands should be sprayed, rubbed vigorously, and run through the hair. Some repellent should be dabbed on the face, neck, and ears, carefully avoiding the eyes; contact wearers should be especially cautious when applying insect repellent.

No-see-ums, which are tiny gnats that abound throughout the tropics of the Americas, are in many regions the single most common source of insect annoyance. They tend to be especially active near sunset and love to feast on the flesh of humans emerging from a bath in a jungle stream. No-see-ums cannot bite through even the thinnest cloth and are usually repelled by Skin So Soft (SSS), sold by Avon. (SSS is not effective against ticks, fleas, flies, and chiggers and offers little protection against mosquitoes.)

SSS should be applied liberally and often to the wrists, knuckles, bare ankles, face, ears, and scalp. Men with full beards seem to be especially troubled by tiny gnats and may benefit by applying small amounts of SSS to the beard area.

How, you may ask, does Skin So Soft work? When the gnats land on the oily surface of skin saturated with Skin So Soft, the oil instantly wicks up their tiny little legs. One of two things then happens: sensing impending doom, the no-see-ums immediately fly away or they stay on your skin and drown before biting.

Insecticides

Permethrin kills or stuns insects that alight upon clothing that has been impregnated with this product. This insecticide is safe, highly effective, and persists even after extensive washing of garments. Permethrin can be purchased as a solution or in an aerosol spray.

Laminated Map

Accurate maps exist for most regions on earth. It pays to search out the best map available and laminate photocopied portions that are relevant to a particular itinerary. (See discussion of topographic maps and satellite images under "Rescue Strategies.")

Machete

A proper machete (long, heavy, and well made) in experienced hands is worth its weight in gold. Also, machetes make excellent gifts and are often more desirable than cash for payment of services.

A 22-inch Collins Military Jungle Machete is a good size; be sure to purchase a sheath. Do not purchase models with a hand guard. Miami Machete Company (*www.miamimachete.com*) makes a high-end model called The Bushmaster. The flimsy machetes sold in most discount stores and sporting shops in the United States are usually not as well made or durable as the machetes sold in developing nations.

Matches or Cigarette Lighter

Waterproof, windproof Hurricane Matches light when damp and stay lit for several seconds even in the strongest wind. Many jungle travelers prefer windproof, burner-coil, butane lighters with a piezo ignition system.

Organizer Bags

See-through organizer bags help reduce clutter and minimize the risk of misplacing small items.

Pen

The Fisher Space Pen (Fisher Pressurized Pen, 711 Yucca Street, Boulder City NE, 89005) writes upside down without pumping, under water and over grease, and in hot and cold temperature extremes. It has an estimated shelf life of over 100 years.

Pocket Tool

A favorite pocket tool for the outdoors enthusiast is the Swiss Army knife. The essential options are a main blade, can opener, bottle opener, flathead screwdriver, and Phillips screwdriver.

Despite the many virtues of the Swiss Army knife, the Leatherman Super Tool is superior for jungle travel and survival. The Leatherman is compact and easy to carry in its belt sheath, features needle-nosed pliers and has 12 useful, locking implements. Since the Leatherman Super Tool came on the market, I've stopped using my Swiss Army knife.

Poly Bottles

High on the list of essential gear are two quart- or liter-sized wide-mouth water bottles made of high-density polyethylene or Lexan polycarbonate.

A 2-ounce, heavy-duty poly bottle comes in handy for carrying a salt and pepper mixture to add flavor to boiled plantains and yucca.

Razor or Battery-Operated Shaver

Both men and women should carry lightweight disposable razors. Most men find that lightweight, AA battery–operated shavers give two shaves a day for up to 2 weeks before requiring a change of batteries. However, men need a manual razor shave every few days because the battery-operated models cannot maintain a uniformly close shave indefinitely.

Spoon

The knife-spoon-fork sets that nest together are unnecessary. Humans do not need a fork to eat. Along with a knife, all that is necessary is a large spoon made of either Lexan polycarbonate or stainless steel.

Sport Sponge

A camp towel, made of microporous material, is lightweight, compact, and mysteriously superabsorbent. It replaces the bulky, hard-to-dry, rot- and odor-prone cotton towel. With the Cascade Designs Pack Towel, or any similar brand, the body and hair can be dried in a fraction of the time it takes with a traditional towel.

Sunglasses

Sunglasses should be polarized with full UV protection. Many travelers prefer sunglasses with red-tinted lenses. Because red is the complement of green, these lenses make the jungle foliage stand out intensely and sharply, giving the illusion of enhanced contrast and depth of field. Eyeglass retainers, such as Chums or Croakies, hold eyeglasses securely during vigorous activity. L.L. Bean sells a rugged, hard-shell sport glasses case made of impact-resistant Lexan polycarbonate.

SunShower

Widely used by boaters, the SunShower produces hot water when set in direct sun for approximately three hours. The Solo SunShower has a three-liter capacity for personal use while trekking. Larger models, up to 10-gallon capacity, are suitable for base camp. I do not pack a SunShower, preferring to take a cleansing dip in a local stream at day's end. For group expeditions, the SunShower is a reasonable item of gear.

Tire Strips

As noted in Chapter 15, there is nothing better suited for making fire in an emergency than thin strips of rubber tire. I suggest you always carry at least six little strips ($\frac{1}{8}$" X $\frac{1}{2}$" X 4"). You can find chunks of shredded truck tires, perfect for slicing into proper strips, along any Interstate highway.

Toilet Paper

American toilet paper is much softer than toilet paper purchased in third-world countries. The traveler should never wipe with jungle leaves. An alternative is to adopt the habit of native people: wipe with the left hand and then rinse the hand with water.

Umbrella

A collapsible umbrella comes in handy in tropical cities and in remote villages when walking from hut to hut. It also offers excellent protection from the sun on canoe or raft trips. Purchase a reflective silver-colored umbrella, not heat-absorbing black.

Watch

Although knowledge of the exact time is generally irrelevant in the third world, it pays to select a good brand that is completely waterproof and has an alarm feature.

Water Carrier

For camp use, the REI Watersack stores up to 3 gallons, has a spigot that opens with just one hand, and weighs only 3.5 oz. empty.

Whistle

A high-quality plastic whistle attached by a lanyard to a belt loop can be used to signal someone in case the trekker strays off the path. REI's Storm Whistle emits an extremely loud sound, purges dirt and water, and is a bright orange color for easy visibility. ACR Electronics, Inc. (*www.acrelectronics.com*) sells the WW-3 Survival Whistle, which weighs a mere 1.4 oz.

Zipper Bags

Heavy-duty zipper freezer bags are excellent for organizing medicines, toiletries, and other small objects. Five each of the gallon, quart, and pint sizes should be brought.

PHOTOGRAPHY

Camera Equipment and Film

Older cameras with mechanical shutters are reliable in regions of high humidity; professionals often choose waterproof Nikonos. Many professional photographers use two lenses in the tropics: a wide-angle to normal zoom and an 80- to 200-mm telephoto zoom. A fast fixed-focal-length lens (*f*1.4) works effectively in the low-light conditions under the jungle canopy. (My preferences are a 24-mm wide-angle $f/2.8$, a 50-mm "normal" $f/1.4$, and a 105-mm macro $f/2.8$.) A UV or skylight filter should be used on each lens to protect the expensive glass; a broken filter can be replaced for a few dollars, while a lens costs hundreds to thousands of dollars.

Water-resistant or waterproof point-and-shoot cameras are worthy of consideration. Although they are less versatile and overall less reliable than mechanical cameras, their convenience offsets these drawbacks.

Whichever camera body and lens combination you choose, the important thing is that you use the equipment and become familiar with it *before you venture into the tropics*. In the low-light conditions of the tropical forest, moderately "fast" film is essential unless a tripod is brought. Kodachrome 200 slide film is an excellent choice. This film produces sharp images and acceptable color saturation. The professional version of Kodachrome 200 is pretested to avoid a magenta cast. For open light situations, consider Fuji Provia 100 film. This film can be pushed 1+ stop to 200 and can be processed in third-world countries.

If you choose to pack a tripod for truly low-light shots, Bogen offers a variety of good economical choices. Gitzo makes a very expensive carbon-fiber model that is exceptionally strong and will not suffer from moisture or abuse. For my style of trekking, I forgo a tripod: it adds too much extra weight and takes up too much space.

From an aesthetic standpoint, your best landscape shots will be in the early morning hours and in the late evening just before sunset. The light hitting the jungle during midday makes for scenes which appear exotic and beautiful to the eye, but dull and uninteresting on film. Except for recording activities of ethnographic interest or truly unusual events, I don't even bother to take my camera out of its case from around 10:00 A.M. to 4:00 P.M. Also, be forewarned that the extreme contrast between the relative dimness under the jungle canopy and scenes where shafts of light stream through from overhead are often too much for any film or light meter to handle. More often than not, such magical scenes will be a great disappointment on film.

One final thought on the subject of film: although the X-ray units at airport security checkpoints are touted as "safe" for regular speed film, why take a chance? To make your passage through airport security swift and hassle-free, keep film in inexpensive lead bags or follow these guidelines:

1. Tell the security guard that you are carrying some high-speed film, above ISO 800. X-ray units *will* ruin high-speed film and airport personnel know that.

2. Remove all your rolls of film from their plastic containers. Put the film, exposed and unexposed, in clear sealable freezer bags so the rolls are clearly visible and present to the security guard for hand inspection.

I pass through airports all over North, Central, and South America several times each year carrying up to 50 rolls of film per trip. I've yet to have any airport official refuse to hand-check film when I have followed the recommendations just given.

Camera Case

Hard-bodied Pelican cases are waterproof and virtually indestructible. The silver-gray color cuts down on heat absorption and is preferred by professional photographers working in hot climates. The cases are ideal for rafting or canoe trips, but bulky for trekking.

Do not store camera equipment in an airtight case with desiccant in a high-moisture environment—equalization problems will cause condensation buildup, particularly in the lenses. On the other hand, if a camera body fails to operate because of excess humidity, sealing it overnight in an airtight compartment with a packet of desiccant may be necessary to get the camera body working again.

PREPARING
MENTALLY FOR
YOUR JOURNEY

CULTURAL AND
PSYCHOLOGICAL FACTORS
Understanding Another Culture
Shamanism
Interacting with Tribal Populations
The Future of Tribal Societies
Psychologic Responses to Unfamiliar Cultures
    and Environments

DYNAMICS OF GROUP TRAVEL IN
EXOTIC ENVIRONMENTS: PITFALLS
AND PERSONALITIES
Groups in Exotic Environments
Group Development
Problems Inherent in Group Trekking
Predictors of Success/Failure in Participants

UNDERSTANDING YOUR
SURROUNDINGS
The Super-Humid Tropical Rainforest
The Saturation-Humidity Cloud Forest
The Tropical Savanna
The Mangrove Swamp

4

CULTURAL AND PSYCHOLOGICAL FACTORS

Understanding Another Culture
Shamanism
Interacting with Tribal
    Populations
The Future of Tribal Societies
Psychologic Responses to
    Unfamiliar Cultures and
    Environments

It is commonly known that many visitors to third-world countries experience culture shock. Not so commonly recognized is the devastating effect of returning to the home culture and succumbing to a disquieting psychological malaise known as *reverse culture-shock.*

Returning travelers often are irked by the discordant noise of our world—the constant background sounds of air-conditioning units, vehicles, radios, and television. Recognizing, perhaps for the first time, that our culture of abundance spills over into vulgar excess is as jarring as the noise; a walk through a modern supermarket can be a wrenching experience.

I recall returning to West Virginia once after trekking great distances over a period of weeks accompanied by Achuar Indians of Ecuador. It had been a physically and emotionally draining trip. Through the miracle of STOL aircraft and commercial jets, I was in the jungle eating plantain and monkey meat one day, and the next day I was back in West Virginia in time to pick up some items at the local supermarket before unpacking at home.

"Say, Dr. Walden," the manager inquired, "how's that little dog of yours?"

"I think Skippy's just fine," I replied. "I just got back in town and I haven't made it home yet."

As we walked down the long aisles whose contents so starkly contrasted with the jungle town markets with their canned tuna and single brand of cereal, the manager kept up a sprightly chatter about Skippy that seemed a little too loud, a little too relentless, to my un-repatriated ears. I wondered what he was driving at.

"I bet that little feller likes ice cream, doesn't he?" he asked.

When we reached the frozen food section, Mr. Johnson reached down into the ice cream bin and scooped up a carton that he thrust triumphantly into my hands.

"It's the new doggie ice cream, Frosty Paws."

It was an ice cream for dogs served in little paper cups. And on the box was the friendly reminder, "It's Not Real Ice Cream, But Your Dog Will *Think* It is!"

"Dr. Walden," the manager said, "you just plop one of those cups down on the ground and that dog of yours—I know he's sure missed you since you've been gone—will lick it up in no time!"

I stared at the carton in my hand. Somewhere inside my head I saw images: of ex-headhunters—faces painted with red achiote—armed with muzzle loaders and machetes walking single-file through the brilliant green forest; there were millisecond bursts of Indian children dying of malaria for lack of 75 cents worth of medicine.

I was not ready for Frosty Paws ice cream for dogs after returning from the Amazon Basin. In fact, years later, I'm *still* not ready for Frosty Paws.

UNDERSTANDING ANOTHER CULTURE

I suspect we never fully understand another culture. Still, there are things one can do to appreciate cultural landmarks. As noted in the previous chapter, back issues of *National Geographic* provide an excellent introduction to the people and places the traveler plans to visit. The care exercised by *National Geographic* authors to get their facts right is legendary: when Loren McIntyre writes that he met and photographed Dr. Reynaldo Mesa in the woebegone Ecuadorian coastal village of Limones, the traveler will discover there really is (or was—alas, he is now deceased) a Dr. Mesa residing in Limones.

The anthropological literature is rich in clues to understanding cultures throughout the world. But, a word of caution: when anthropologists were in the business of describing peoples and cultures (descriptive anthropology), there was exceptional accuracy; what they reported was pretty much what you were likely to encounter if you visited the society in question. Alas, anthropologists have described, measured, and photographed human beings around the globe with such success they have run out of people to describe, measure, and photograph. Lamentably, they now seem to focus their energies in the arena of interpretive anthropology. When anthropologists get into the business of delving into the "meaning" of symbols and myth and substitute their revelations for fact, their credibility enters the tenuous realm of psychoanalytic theory and religion: it must be accepted on faith—a leap some of us are unwilling to take. Still, in their interpretive ramblings, nuggets of true gold will be discovered by the diligent prospector.

Adjusting to Cultural Differences

Despite the time and effort spent attuning yourself to cultural differences, some things simply take getting used to. It has taken me years, for example, to come to terms with the moment of departure when embarking on a trek with Indian guides and porters. Even though we may be away for weeks at a time, we simply walk out of the village as though expecting to return within the next hour. There are no last-minute embraces or tearful scenes; no one calls out, "Hey guys, have a great trip, but be careful—it's a jungle out there!" What's with these people? Don't they . . . *care*?

Of course they do. But what might be mistaken for some sort of societal emotional blunting is in actuality just the Amazonian Indian way: they don't see the need to emote in public. Goodbyes were said in private; everyone in the village knows who is leaving on the trip and the risks involved—so what's the point of making a major production out of it? And, when we return home at journey's end, more often than not, few individuals acknowledge our arrival beyond lingering a few seconds longer as they glance our way—no high-fiving in this crowd! It takes time to feel at home with these cultural dissimilarities.

Keep an Open Mind

It helps to keep an open mind. Once my Shuar friend Daniel introduced me to a legendary headman living on the Pastaza River.

"He's a very powerful man, Doctor." Grinning, he added, "And he has five wives!"

We walked down the trail a ways and Daniel asked, "How many wives do you have?"

"One," I said.

"Only one? Why is that?" he asked.

"Well, in my country it is against the law to have more than one wife at a time."

For about five minutes, Daniel remained silent as we continued trucking down the trail. Finally he stopped and with a pitying look in his eyes turned to me and said, "Bad luck."

Infanticide

Travelers who have the privilege of spending time with jungle-dwelling populations will find much to admire in the lives of indigenous peoples throughout the world. In some cultures, however, various facets of tribal life lend a discordant note and remind us that all cultures have their unpleasant aspects.

In a few tribal societies, infanticide is still practiced. Often, the first or second of twins (depending on the customs of a particular tribe) and deformed newborns are killed. In some tribes, when the firstborn is a female instead of the more prized male, the decision may be made to kill the child at birth.

Intertribal Warfare, Revenge Killings, Homicide

Although the rates may be significantly lower or slightly higher on a regional basis, the literature is fairly clear that those who observed certain indigenous populations during their first sustained contact with the outside world found a high background level of intertribal warfare, revenge killings, and homicide. Reliable data, painstakingly gathered by anthropologists, indicates a fairly consistent 30 to 40 percent death rate in some regions of Amazonia among adult males as the result of violence. (Rates as high as 60 percent have been documented.)

Interestingly, after contact most groups rapidly abandon generations of warfare and violence. Influences, including Christian missionization, schools, and sports—especially intervillage soccer tournaments—have been credited with the transformation to more pacific lifestyles. In the case of some tribal groups, truces after mass killings are tenuous at best. In fact, the Achuar and, especially, the Waorani Indians of the Amazon Basin have, after decades of relative peace, recently renewed old patterns of violence—fortunately, on a limited scale. Readers who wish to learn more about the conditions surrounding violence in tribal populations should consult the fascinating and informative text *Waorani: The Contexts of Violence and War,* authored by Clayton and Carole Robarchek.

If you disregard the theories of squabbling academicians—much of which strikes me as political correctness gone awry—and *ask the Indians themselves,* you will find the preoccupation with warfare and homicide is attributed to revenge killings (vendettas), sexual disputes, and shamanism.

SHAMANISM

A shaman is a man or woman who, in any tribal society, intercedes between humans and spirits in the context of health versus sickness. The shaman is often the keeper of tribal traditions and may be thought of as the intermediary between the individual or community and the supernatural world.

To understand the role of the shamanist healer, it is important to know that in tribal societies, particularly in the Americas, disease due to natural causes is a foreign concept. Virtually all illness and accidents have a magic origin and occur, for example, as the result of an invisible missile shot by a sorcerer (or spirit) or because the patient's soul has been kidnapped or has fled.

The shaman, the healer, works by removing the object that causes the illness or removing the magic substance. In the case of a soul that is lost, the shaman can send his own spirit out to retrieve the victim's soul and put it back in the body of the victim. The shaman accomplishes this feat by transforming into a jaguar. The jaguar-shaman, like the actual jaguar, is able to see in the dark, go long distances, and roam through the forest in the night to find and retrieve wandering or kidnapped souls.

Throughout the world, shamans put themselves in a trancelike state in order to see and contact the supernatural through fasting, flagellation, sensory deprivation, meditation, and ritual dancing and drumming. Plant hallucinogens are an easy and fast way to achieve visions and a supernatural experience. Certain psychoactive drugs that come from plants characteristically make users feel they have taken a "trip" and have voyaged outside their bodies. The shaman describes the experience as a "journey."

Becoming a Shaman

Often the individual who becomes a shaman gets a *call* from the spirit world, often in the form of a sudden vision. A period of training, lasting from months to 10 years and, more often than not, requiring complete sexual abstinence, is required.

The shaman's sing-song chant has a truly hypnotic quality, the rhythm broken occasionally by the frequent rustling of shaken, dried palm fronds or the rattle of dried seeds. By the dim glow of embers from a log fire or a cheap rag-wicked lantern made from a tin can, you can study at close range the intensity of his efforts. He is away, far away as he struggles to discover the evil force lodged within the patient's prostrate body.

Village medicine men usually do not announce their profession, but I have learned to spot the powerful ones by their circumspect behavior and an ill-defined distant look in their eyes. Let me share with you clues to recognizing these remarkable individuals:

Age Most shamans are older men simply because cultural forces (schools and missionaries) are making the arduous apprenticeship leading to mastery of Shamanism less of a desirable calling to young men than it was in the past.

Behavior Medicine men seem detached or disconnected. I suspect their frequent use of extremely potent hallucinogens is partially responsible. I have, by the way, only rarely known medicine men to speak or act in a way that could be interpreted as openly hostile or even discourteous; yet, there is something in their manner that is distinctly guarded.

Eyes Their eyes are often bloodshot. This is nothing more than a reflection of consuming copious amounts of hallucinogens and alcohol, being exposed to tobacco smoke (in certain cultures), and staying awake night after night during healing ceremonies.

Language Spoken Medicine men are often the only men in the village who do not (or will not) speak the dominant language of the country.

Dwelling They often live quite a distance away from the main village or across the river from the main concentration of huts. If you know your plants, you may be able to recognize psychoactive species that make up the shaman's pharmacopeia growing in the yard or in a nearby garden.

Subjective They simply *look* like witch doctors. I know it when I see it . . . you will too with experience.

INTERACTING WITH TRIBAL PEOPLES

Fish and guests in three days are stale.

John Lyly (1519)

Wearing Out Your Welcome

When traveling in regions with minimal outside contact, there is a magic window of welcome which seems to last about 3 days. After that, unless you have a good reason for remaining in their midst, the newness of your presence wears off and you may find that you are avoided, ignored, or encouraged to move on. After 3 days, the risk of physical harm increases when residing among overtly antagonistic populations.

Patience

The rhythms of life are different in traditional cultures. Patience, a concept with minimal currency in our modern lives, must be appreciated and mastered if you are to have success in your dealings with tribesmen. You have a timetable that makes sense to you; it makes no sense in the context of tribal life.

Appropriate Eye Contact

Eye contact is a type of probing. Sometimes it is a sexual probing. Unless the male traveler knows the culture well, it is best to avoid making direct and prolonged eye contact with females. Tribesmen may get wrong ideas or, as can be the case, see the eye contact for exactly what it is: checking out the local girls. In some populations this can be a hazardous, even deadly, game.

Gender Issues

Generally, women put strangers at ease; men don't. Whatever the reason, if you are male and plan to visit a tribal population that has infrequent outside contact, including a female from your own culture as a traveling companion is worth serious consideration: you will be perceived as less of a threat by tribesmen and may find it is much easier to establish rapport.

Throughout the Neotropics, travelers who are male generally have ready access to masculine activities but are often excluded from observing women's activities. Women from our culture are always welcome in the world of native women and, curiously, may be accepted as observers in masculine activities and rituals from which native women are excluded.

Interpreting Tone of Voice and Facial Expressions

We are culturally programmed to read meaning into tone of voice, facial expression, and body language. When interacting with individuals from tribal societies, be cautious before interpreting the intentions of someone based on these familiar, but sometimes misleading, cues.

During years of negotiations with Shuar and Achuar Indians of Ecuador, I never ceased to be amazed at the seeming disconnectedness between an Indians' tone of voice and facial expressions and the eventual outcome of deliberations. Early on in my interactions with these Amerindians, I often had the feeling there was wholesale opposition to any request or proposal. Whether the issue was something as simple as procuring a guide and porters for overland treks, or as intricate as a planning session for village health promotion, there seemed to be a phase during which a village spokesperson's demeanor suggested we were going nowhere fast. Often I found myself on the receiving end of a long harangue in which everything from past misdeeds of outsiders to inclement weather was given as reasons why no one had the slightest intention of cooperating.

As time passed I learned that dour expressions and borderline hostility were almost always nothing more than a bargaining strategy. Eventually I realized the interminable speeches served as terrific diversions for a population for whom things moved on a time frame that had little to do with my wristwatch. My evolution of understanding the "Indian" way of coming to an agreement was aided considerably by advice from a frequent traveling companion and Shuar friend, Daniel Cashindo. When things seemed hopelessly bogged down and I began to think of places to be, things to do, and schedules to keep, Daniel would sense my frustration and whisper to me, "It will work out—he is just talking. He will talk for another hour or so and then he will stop and the headman will agree to your proposal. Just drink a bowl or two of chicha and let him say what he has to say." And, sure enough, nine times out of ten, things would work out exactly as Daniel predicted.

THE FUTURE OF TRIBAL SOCIETIES

Increasing inroads of modern technological civilization are rapidly destroying primitive societies the world over. Roads, air transport, forest devastation, increased missionary activity, wars, and even heightened tourism are all contributing to this loss.

Richard Evans Schultes, *Plants of the Gods*

The external forces emphasized by Schultes are only part of the equation explaining the changes that threaten to overwhelm every tribal population on earth. In my opinion, internal pressures are an underappreciated and underpublicized element. Let's call it the Aluminum

Pot Theory of Inexorable Change. You are an indigenous housewife. You have at your disposal various-sized items of pottery that serve as containers used in preparation, serving, and storage of food and drink. These vessels, decorated with patterns that identify them as coming from your own hands, are perfectly symmetrical, lovely to the eye, and would qualify as works of art suitable for display in a museum collection.

Each piece takes hours to produce, requiring patience and remarkable skill. First, you have to find a source of suitable clay, extract it from the ground, and haul it back to your village. You add tempering materials, sand, and fine grit or ash from the *caraipe* tree, then moisten the clay to the precise consistency necessary for coiling. Then you roll the coils out and, coil by coil, build the pot up. With great skill you produce the exact shape and desired thinness of the sides. After a few days of drying, you add designs that include storytelling elements related to the life of you and your family. You fire the piece and apply a resin.

Unfortunately, a small bump or too-rapid heating causes a crack to appear in the pot, and its days as a receptacle for liquids cease. You must make another pot. But since this is all you know in your experience within your tribal culture, you aren't particularly bothered to repeat the cycle: make pot—use pot—break pot.

One day, your husband returns from a hunting expedition with a gift. While visiting a distant village that has contact with a Catholic mission where trade-goods may be obtained, he exchanged a hunting dog for a shiny aluminum pot. You soon discover this lightweight pot is virtually indestructible and totally immune to damage from variance in heat. Because the weight is negligible, you can carry it with you when making annual treks to visit relatives or for hunting and fishing expeditions. You will never again go back to using the museum-quality clay pots that have served your people for generations. Furthermore, every woman in your village wants a pot just like yours and *no husband will have any peace until he provides his wife with a similar aluminum pot.* The floodgates have opened: the culture is changed forevermore.

Can you imagine clearing acres of land with stone axes? Traveling through the forest without a steel machete? Traveling upstream in a canoe using pole and paddle for days on end when an outboard motor can make the same run in a couple of hours? In my experience, all newly contacted groups go through predictable, sequential stages of acculturation and adoption of modern technologies and those stages vary only slightly in the time line. You can predict with certainty that newly contacted villages will rapidly acquire aluminum pots, axes, machetes, and cloth, followed by battery-powered radios, outboard motors, and chainsaws. It takes only a few years to make the transition from walking barefoot and essentially naked with the fore-skin of your penis tied to your waist to wearing blue jeans and Nikes.

It is inevitable that contacts will occur with increasing frequency, even in the most isolated regions of the tropics, as a result of population movements into those areas and as a result of internal pressures as the indigenous peoples themselves seek goods and services from the outside world. Cultural change also is inevitable; to think otherwise is counterproductive for those whose desire to assist indigenous populations rises above naive, selfish romanticism.

Health and Disease in Tribal Societies

Malnutrition definitely plays a major role in the health picture of native populations throughout tropical Africa and India. By contrast, jungle-dwelling Indians of Central and South America have rarely suffered from malnutrition. And of those who do, it is often those who have the most contact with the outside world. In the past few years, increasing migratory pressures driven by government-sponsored colonization programs have led to intensified hunting and fishing resulting in a depletion of reserves of wild game and fish. For the first time, I am beginning to see malnutrition among some Amerindian populations inhabiting lowland forests.

Malaria is hyperendemic throughout many regions inhabited by tribal peoples of the world and is a major cause of mortality among all age groups. The prevalence of hepatitis B among some tribal groups (the Yanomami of Venezuela and Brazil, for example) is extremely high.

Tuberculosis is often a major cause of morbidity and mortality among tribal populations. Measles can be a killer among unvaccinated Amerindian populations and represents a serious threat, as do the myriad sexually transmitted diseases that have reached explosive proportions as some groups experience increasing and unavoidable contact with the outside world.

Homicide resulting from ongoing intratribal warfare, revenge killings, and massacres of Indian populations in South America (by gold miners and land developers) are probably more common than the anthropological literature and news reports would indicate.

PSYCHOLOGIC RESPONSES TO UNFAMILIAR CULTURES AND ENVIRONMENTS

What better way of sifting out what is essential from what is not in all that fashions your social personality than to be suddenly transplanted into an exotic tribe where you are out of your depth in everything except yourself?

Philippe Descola

Culture Shock

Culture shock describes the physical and emotional discomfort one suffers when coming to live in another country or place different from the place of origin. Those who suffer the frustration and anxiety of culture shock may develop symptoms of sadness, loneliness, insomnia (or the desire to sleep too much), depression, irritability, and an unwillingness to interact with others. (See *edweb.sdsu.edu/people/CGuanipa/cultshok.*)

These are the stages of culture shock:

Stage I Often called the "honeymoon" stage. This is a time of near euphoria. Everything in the new culture is exciting . . . remarkable revelations are to be found around every corner! "Where have these wonderful people been all my life?"

Stage II Reality begins to set in: things aren't so cheery after all. Strong feelings of dissatisfaction with the new culture are common.

Stage III Some understanding of the new culture takes place; there is a feeling of psychological balance.

Stage IV The individual develops an appreciation of both the good and bad elements of the new culture.

Even among individuals trained to anticipate culture shock in their work overseas, it still is a common occurrence. So how can you prevent it?

Preventing Culture Shock

- Travel with someone from your own ethnic background; it helps keep things in perspective. If this is not possible, try to maintain contact with your ethnic group by phone, ham radio, mail, or e-mail.

- Be patient! Adapting to another culture takes time.

- Don't try too hard to "fit in" or attain instant mastery of cultural "do's and don'ts." You will *never* fully understand all of the cultural taboos of a truly alien culture. Fortunately, most people recognize that outsiders are fairly clueless, and they are not nearly as offended by social gaffes as most people fear. Of course, there are notable exceptions to this generality where an offending act or statement can have dire consequences. A brief review of almost any anthropological text on the culture you plan to visit will help you avoid potentially catastrophic blunders.

- Actively pursue a hobby, especially one that takes advantage of local conditions. Birdwatching or macrophotography, for example, are excellent activities that will keep you occupied and enhance your appreciation of the local flora and fauna.

- Learn as much as you can about the local culture; in the process you will learn much about yourself and the relativity of your own ethnic beliefs.

- Learn the language.

- Be curious about life in general.

- Maintain a sense of humor!

- Keep an open mind. Make the extra effort to maintain flexibility and tolerance. Curiosity, humor, and openmindedness are critical to intercultural adjustment.

Repatriation Stress/Reverse Culture Shock

Travelers, especially those who spend extensive amounts of time living intimately with tribal groups, find it disconcerting to discover that it is not culture shock that so jangles the psyche. It is reverse culture shock: a sense of alienation and isolation from one's own society when returning home. *Repatriation stress*, or *home culture despondency*, characterizes the fact that after an intense experience overseas in a tribal setting, coming home is rough; home seems weird.

Prevention and Treatment of Repatriation Stress

Recognition of the early symptoms of repatriation stress can be a first step in prevention. Those who suffer from this common condition experience the following: general moodiness; detachment and strained relationships; feelings of guilt over our culture of material excess; a judgmental attitude toward others who are unabashedly enjoying the good life; and overt depression (insomnia or excessive sleep, overeating or decreased appetite, irritability, disinterest, feelings of worthlessness, and inability to experience pleasure).

Fortunately, the unpleasant emotional fallout of repatriation stress generally passes in weeks or months as the victim reconnects with the home culture. During the transient phase of bothersome symptoms, reassurance or talk sessions may be helpful. A sympathetic coworker, friend, or trained professional who will simply allow the sufferer to ventilate ("reintegrative catharsis") may be all that is required to facilitate the shift in cultural identity.

Culture Entrancement

Be they gold miners or missionaries or anthropologists, they warn themselves; keep one foot always in "your" world, don't allow yourself to be completely overwhelmed by the Indians, don't go too far into their terrain. Getting back might become very difficult.

Geoffrey O'Connor

Exotic environments by their very nature prime our consciousness for illusory interpretations of events. If you spend enough time in the jungle, you will eventually experience something very strange—something that seems plausible only on a supernatural plane. It may be something you see (or think you see!) or an overwhelming sense of the unworldly. For a moment, the spectral reality of tribesmen makes about as much sense as your own Western, science-based perspective. Let me give just one example of an odd occurrence that, at the time, seemed utterly fantastic but, of course, on reflection had a perfectly logical explanation. I will not even try to explain the anteater that disappeared—literally in the blink of an eye—in front of several trekkers on an outing in Ecuador.

On my first true expedition, through inexperience and some measure of stupidity, I found myself one night in a kayak in the swollen Cayapa River tied off to a branch some 15 feet up in a riverside tree. Because of the near-terror of the situation, the uncertainty of the outcome, and self-incrimination that I had put a companion at risk of dying, it was difficult to maintain a dispassionate state of mind. Sudden surges of water, the frequent and ominous sound of huge tree trunks crashing, and the misery of a constant rain of biting insects and debris from higher up in the tree added to the anxiety. When combined with a total lack of sleep throughout the night, these events made me feel that I was living in a waking nightmare; the unreality of the situation made it easy to misinterpret the mostly auditory cues of impending doom.

Just before daybreak, when my companion and I were totally drained, physically and emotionally, we heard, from far away, a low moaning. I decided that it was some freakish effect of the racing current or that my mind was just playing tricks. Time passed. The sound returned, a little louder this time. Then I remembered the Indians had mentioned the "roaring monster" that, when aroused by lightning and thunder, howled its displeasure. I heard the moan again, much louder, more drawn out and . . . closer. Wedged into a folding kayak, tethered some 15 feet up in a tree, bobbing precariously in raging waters that rushed through the potential death trap of a narrow and steep canyon, *anything* seemed possible.

Years later, the local Indians were induced to visit the area of the roaring monster—a region they had for generations absolutely refused to traverse—and the source of the sound was revealed: a waterfall dropping onto the hollowed-out stone of the stream bed below.

When It's Time to Go Home

Over the last few months my curiosity has become much less keen . . . dissipated in day-to-day banalities, the exotic has lost the fresh appeal of its mystery. It is time to pack my bags.

Philippe Descola

Often we embark on a project driven by some compelling emotion that defies logic but, at the time, feels right and irresistible. As can happen with any passion, one day you wake up and the feeling just isn't there anymore.

If you have a real job to do, obviously you must carry on and complete the task. If what you are doing is more for your own personal jollies than to fulfill some cosmic imperative, however, call it a day and head home when you run out of steam and enthusiasm. Interestingly, you may discover, as I have, that in a relatively short time, the old urge resurfaces and you are making plans to return.

5

DYNAMICS OF GROUP TRAVEL IN EXOTIC ENVIRONMENTS: PITFALLS AND PERSONALITIES

Groups in Exotic Environments
Group Development
Problems in Group Travel
Predictors of Success/Failure in
Participants

In the summer of 1972, I joined a tour group on a hiking trip in the Bolivian Andes. Today, it would have been a more organized eco-tour type affair (pretrip readings, lectures in the field, shared environmental philosophies); then it was mostly a group of wandering souls who happened to chance upon a notice tacked onto a low-budget hotel bulletin board promising "Good Vibes" and "True Adventure."

At first, things went swimmingly: everyone was on their best behavior and the beauty of the surroundings was truly breathtaking. After day 2, however, it became apparent that there were tensions between a husband–wife duo in our little band of trekkers. Initially, there were subtle digs by one spouse or the other; then more pointed, sarcastic comments surfaced. By day 4, some within the group had chosen sides with one or the other of the squabbling pair.

As we ascended into ever more rarefied air, the feuding couple ceased all pretense of mutual respect and resorted to name-calling. On day 6, as we trudged along at 15,000 feet elevation, the two were at it nonstop on the theme of infidelity. By this time, any support from other members had long vanished ("they're *both* assholes") and other members in the group pointedly moved their tents away from the couple at each night's campsite.

On the morning of day 8, as the sun peeked over the eastern cordillera and light streamed down onto our campsite on the high altiplano, we were awakened not by some Andean songbird trilling in the distance, but by a proverbial blood-curdling scream! Several men and women, some wearing only underpants and boots, some only boots (it was not a pretty sight), rushed from their tents to investigate. We crested the small knoll that separated the main campsite from the couples' spot and gazed down. The man was on one side of a brook and the woman on the other, hurling stones at each other's heads. The man, having the better aim it seemed, had connected at least once; blood was streaming down the woman's face.

At that point the Bolivian tour organizer had had enough and ordered a porter to escort the couple off the mountain.

Remarkably consistent emotional and behavioral reactions occur when groups travel into remote regions where there are few safety nets. The following discussion is designed to aid trip organizers and expedition participants anticipate the many problems inherent in group travel in order to take preventive or corrective action in a timely manner.

GROUPS IN EXOTIC ENVIRONMENTS

Exotic environments are characterized by severe climates, danger, limited facilities and supplies, isolation from family and friends, and enforced interaction with others. Individuals engaged in a variety of activities in exotic settings commonly report motivational decline, a dip in intellectual performance, mood swings, and increased bodily complaints.

People living in extreme environments universally experience interpersonal conflict, tensions, and feelings of hostility among group members. A recent near-mutiny at an Australian Antarctic winter base revealed how leadership style, an exclusive (sexual) relationship, group dynamics, power cliques, tension, and isolation led to "mob culture" as 14 expeditioners defied an inflexible leader they could not stand. By the time a mediator was dispatched from Australia, the situation was beyond salvaging.

Studies on space travel and simulated space travel show that within a surprisingly short time, interpersonal tensions mount, group cohesiveness starts to erode, and scapegoating of unpopular crew members begins. Undersea experiments, designed to see how people might react to the confinement and isolation of future space travel, showed that as the missions progressed, crew members began to withdraw and increasingly craved privacy; spiraling tension and outbursts of anger followed. Similar trends have been reported in the Mercury, Apollo, and Skylab flights, as well as Soviet space flights.

Experience has shown that wilderness expeditions often fail because leaders neglect the dynamics between group members. The inability to resolve conflict is a well-documented, recurring theme in unsuccessful Himalayan expeditions. Skills that maintain a supportive social climate over time are critical if the group is to weather the changing conditions of wilderness trips.

Why do things tend to go astray when groups venture into strange environments? *Environmental causation* theories suggest that, as a result of exotic conditions, capable and well-adjusted people begin to show signs of maladjustment. Alternatively, *environmental drift* explanations hint that exotic environments attract people who already have psychological liabilities. There probably is some truth to both concepts.

GROUP DEVELOPMENT

Expeditioners can avoid some of the pitfalls that come with group dynamics by understanding the phases all groups pass through over time. Tuckman's Theory of Developmental Sequence in Small Groups is an attractive model that, at the very least, represents a framework for discussing how groups form, change, and adjust. New groups go through four different stages whereby members establish the structure of the task for which they convene (*forming*), emotionally react to the demands of the task (*storming*), negotiate intra- and intergroup roles to develop group cohesion (*norming*), and resolve role conflicts and move on to the successful completion of the task (*performing*).

Individuals and groups can get bogged down anywhere along the way, especially in the storming phase when the "newness" of the group has worn off. Jordan likens this emotional phase of opposition and conflict to a teenager breaking away from parents. She recommends the leader address these normal feelings of anger, frustration, and irritation with the entire group with the aim of working through the issues.

Cashel studied the pattern of mood states of wilderness course participants over a period of 3 years. Consistently, she found that day 4 was a pivotal day in a wilderness expedition with a high level of confusion, fatigue, anger, depression, and tension. Unless disenchantment with the expedition occurs or group commitments are not fulfilled, this period of conflict passes and groups move into a constructive work phase.

PROBLEMS IN GROUP TRAVEL

Leadership

Leaders exercise their influence for the following purposes: to meet challenges posed from without, to set goals, to maintain group harmony, and to interpret conditions that are threatening to the group. Those who wish to head expeditions into wilderness areas should recognize that a number of things can invalidate the authority of the group leader, erode confidence, and contribute to poor, or even failed, leadership.

Ambiguous Authority

Just as ships at sea do not run under the command of a committee, expeditions do not run smoothly when authority is too diffuse. In other words, there should be no question as to who is in charge and how the chain of command flows.

Ambiguous Goals

Ambiguous goals, or worse, false representation of mission and purpose, also contribute to failed leadership. A recent expedition in the Amazon Basin was billed as a scientific trip but proved to be little more than an adventure for the amusement of the wealthy organizer. A thin layer of science was added to the project only to ease the process of obtaining travel permits from the host government. Research scientists became rightly indignant upon discovering they were nothing more than props.

If the goal is to have an adventure, say so! If the goal is scientific, say so. And if the goal is to have a combination of adventure and science, make that clear to participants. It is always a mistake to bill an undertaking as a scientific venture if, in fact, it is just a publicity stunt or adventure-for-the-hell-of-it. And there is absolutely nothing wrong with forays into wilderness just for the hell of it; what is wrong is to misrepresent the real intent to participants.

Lack of Experience

Lack of experience is the usual reason for poor and ineffectual planning. Neophyte group leaders often don't recognize how much time and energy it takes to address the numerous details that are requisite for a successful wilderness venture.

Lack of experience also can lead to a significant underestimation of the time required to traverse unknown or difficult jungle terrain, especially during the rainy season. As I note elsewhere, after 2 or 3 weeks of travel in remote jungle areas, the general health of expedition participants unavoidably deteriorates.

Ethnographic Issues

Thundering ignorance of ethnography on the part of organizers and leaders can readily bring into question the seriousness of group leaders and undermine their credibility.

A few years ago, I was the physician for a 21-member team that retraced Teddy Roosevelt's trouble-plagued 1914 descent of the River of Doubt (Rio Duvida) in Brazil. Our highly publicized rafting expedition, rumored to have set the organizers back some $200,000, was portrayed in pretrip articles in newspapers and on television as a passage through virtually untouched wilderness—a region inhabited by minimally contacted, *possibly dangerous*, Brazilian Indians. After all the media hype, we found the supposedly pristine jungle crisscrossed with logging roads; trails made by gold-seeking *garimpeiros* paralleled the river for miles at a stretch. When we actually made contact with the Indians they were watching *Star Trek* on generator-powered television via a satellite dish! Better research by the trip organizers would have ferreted out the modern realities of life along the river.

Bogus Credentials

Truth is one of the great gifts of the sea. You cannot persuade yourself . . . that the wind is not blowing when it is, or that a cabin with half a foot of water in it is dry, or that a dragging anchor holds. Everywhere the sea is a teacher of truth.

Hilaire Belloc

Wilderness, too, is a teacher of truth.

The wilderness expedition leader is, in many ways, like the skipper of a small yacht tossed by uncaring storm waves at sea: bluff counts for nothing. To the noxious plants, venomous reptiles, and insects of the jungle, posturing is irrelevant. Wilderness can be the ultimate lie detector and comeuppance.

For those who would be group leaders and expedition organizers: don't pretend to be what you are not. In a dangerous environment the pretense of jungle savvy cannot be sustained. If you lack significant experience in the ways of the jungle, hire someone who is experienced and have that person join the expedition as an advisor. Be sure the other members understand the role of this experienced advisor.

Gender Issues

There are essentially two schools of thought on the introduction of females into group undertakings that have, traditionally, been all male:

Destabilizing/Stabilizing Effects of Females   Some studies indicate alpha male behaviors seem to occur with increased frequency in mixed-gender outings. Other studies, however, indicate females express more positive effect than males and may have an important function for the reduction of tension in the group. Space simulation missions often characterize women as peacemakers. Research-oriented physician mountaineers such as Charles Houston and Peter Hackett echo the peacekeeper role. In addition, women as team managers are often superior to men in their ability to broker different sides of an argument.

Conversational differences may play a role in the stabilizing effects of females. Systematic observations, starting in childhood, confirm the tendency of men and women to have different conversational styles. Females tend to use words as a bridge; males are more inclined to use words as weapons or instruments of dominance.

Exclusive Relationships   A number of expedition leaders privately note that individuals who have a sexual relationship form a team within a team. Such exclusive relationships create a bond that makes objectivity virtually impossible and poisons the dynamics of the group experience. Although it would *seem* easy for two intelligent people to think rationally enough to compartmentalize their emotional attachment and do what is best for the group, such is not the case. Maybe it's just a simple fact of the human condition: in any contest between brains and glands, put your money on glands; you'll win every time!

Anecdotally, there is a *lot* of support for the notion that the tropics somehow engender sexual activity. The experience of those of us who spend essentially all our wilderness time in the hot zones, as opposed to those whose preferences are for high altitude and freezing environments, leads inescapably to the conclusion that group tensions brought on by sex or the pursuit of sex are much more an issue in the tropics than in colder climates.

What can an expedition leader do to avert problems arising from raging libidos? Probably not a lot! For what it's worth, however, my approach has been to meet with the team members before actually heading into the jungle and discuss the strong possibility that romances may spring up during the course of the trip. Then I state my own feelings on the subject: 1) it doesn't add a whole lot to the cross-cultural experience when natives witness how we "do it," and 2) the risk of serious dissension within the group is very real when exclusive relationships develop. The group is encouraged to verbalize how they plan to deal with the issue when (not if) it comes up.

Drugs

Cocaine not uncommonly causes anxiety and mood swings and has been implicated in heart arrhythmias, heart attacks, seizures, and strokes: not exactly the sort of things one wants to deal with in a wilderness setting. Marijuana use can lead to mood alteration with either euphoria or depression, a sense of dissociation from surroundings, depersonalization, anxiety, and panic. Marijuana adversely affects coordination for 24 hours. Jungle log bridges are difficult enough to traverse; why increase the already significant risk of falls and injury?

On trips I organize and lead, I make it very clear that the use of recreational drugs will not be tolerated. Anyone who chooses to break this rule will be on the next plane home. No second chance. It's as simple as that.

Alcohol can be a mixed blessing. When an expedition has gone well, a beer-bust can solidify group unity and help participants unwind. However, in the setting of preexisting anger and hostility, alcohol is one of the quickest ways to ensure that a trip will come unraveled. As the old Spanish saying goes, "When the wine goes in, the truth comes out." Alcohol can unmask and release pent-up resentment and frustration toward individual team members, cliques, and, often, the leader. I have seen expeditioners come to blows during the course of what started off as a few friendly beers at a resupply point.

Jungle Companions to Avoid

Boneheads (the Terminally Dense) Some people just don't get it. Back in their home culture, millions of people can screw up day after day, never learn from their mistakes, and just keep right on truckin'. In the wilderness, however, certain mistakes can be very costly.

Fortunately, boneheads generally create mischief that is more nuisance than catastrophic. I recall the first evening meal of a 6-week rafting expedition when we discovered all 20 loaves of bread and dozens of boxes of crackers reeked of gasoline fumes that no amount of airing out could remedy. Unfortunately, the supply coordinator had packed the food in waterproof containers along with leaking cans of gasoline.

After 2 weeks of grueling white-water rapids, we eagerly looked forward to fresh goodies at a resupply point. We had used our trusty satellite telephone on three separate occasions to remind the quartermaster to be sure to pack the food supplies *away from the gasoline*. As we shuttled items from the resupply truck to the rafts it was discovered that, once again, all the bread and crackers were packed adjacent to the gasoline!

The only good thing about boneheads is their predictability; they can be counted on to make the same errors in judgment over and over. The wise leader will keep such people away from decision-making that requires savvy.

Space Cadets (the Terminally Weird) These people are often loners who gravitate to unusual, out-of-the-way adventure travel: garden-variety nuts or individuals with chronic, substantial psychiatric pathology. I am amazed at the number of phone calls I get from people of this ilk who want to go on trips into jungle regions. I usually get clues during the course of the initial phone conversation. If you are a group leader and alarms start going off somewhere inside your head, it is usually wise to follow your gut instincts. On the two occasions I did not follow my instincts the individuals proved to be disastrous choices.

Hazardous enterprises in exotic locations seem to attract people with situational problems: folks on the rebound trying to recover from personal quandaries. Divorce and the breakup of long-term relationships figure prominently in this subset of would-be trekkers.

Sometimes, when we face personal problems (and, don't we all?), communing with nature is therapeutic. Being in a group setting in extreme wilderness is another matter; people with major emotional problems will not get better in an exotic, wilderness environment.

Gung-ho Guys Here I'm referring to the take-the-lead-on-the-trail male; the fellow who, on his first trip into serious wilderness, dashes ahead of the native guides and, for a while, sets a blistering pace.

I've not seen any research data on who these guys are but, from my own experience, I have encountered a number of men who fit into this category who either have a background of successful elite military training (Green Beret, Rangers) or have intense religious beliefs. Such individuals think that through sheer willpower, or through prayer, anything can be overcome and mastered. Unfortunately, you can't will yourself to immediate acclimatization to the heat and humidity of the tropical rainforest any more than you can will yourself to rapid acclimatization to the effects of low oxygen at high altitude.

My approach has been to let these men wear themselves down to a point just short of physical exhaustion, and thus a more manageable state. If heat exhaustion or heat shock loom, I take them aside and discuss their behavior and the possible health consequences; it helps to remind them how unsexy they will look in a body bag.

Ennui

It usually begins about 10 days into the trip. At first there are mutterings of dissatisfaction with one thing or another, often food (What! Monkey arms, *again?*). Folks are wondering out loud how The Simpsons are getting along and begin expressing regret that there is no junk mail delivery in the jungle. The heat and humidity, accompanied by the annoying and unrelenting drone of insects, induces a state of sapped energy that manifests itself as a sort of group weariness. Daily, as the sun reaches its apogee, you can feel IQ points flaking off like dandruff.

This is a signal that people really are beginning to tire of the jungle experience; getting back to nature has about run its course. During such times, it helps to schedule a day of unfettered goofing off. You can begin thinking of all the superb food and cold beer that will be consumed at the coming-out-of-the-jungle party in the first town you come to on your way back to the big city. If alcohol is available . . . this is the time to use it!

Too Many People, Too Much Junk

All sort of problems, especially injuries, seem to increase logarithmically when you get beyond 7 to 10 members in a wilderness group. As noted in Chapter 3, the idea is to travel as light as possible. Even experienced trip organizers may succumb to the siren call of the latest must-have gizmo. Excess gear only adds complication and misery: just because someone makes it doesn't mean you need it. The gear listed in the section on preparing for the jungle will do the job. *Overdependence* on high-tech communications gear for safety backup is a mistake: anything electronic eventually breaks or mysteriously ceases to function just when you need it most.

PREDICTORS OF SUCCESS/FAILURE IN PARTICIPANTS

When it comes to criteria for selecting or rejecting applicants on wilderness trips, much more is known about how to exclude people who are liable to react badly than how to choose people of exceptional psychological health. An applicant's attitude, sense of humor, previous record of success or failure in a wilderness venture, past history of counseling or psychological treatment, and the leader's intuition all play a role in predicting success or failure in jungle travel.

Attitude

A positive attitude means so much in our day-to-day lives; doubly so in situations where there is heightened physical and psychological stress. Individuals with a bad attitude are unlikely to take a miraculous turn for the better in the demanding environment of the tropical rainforest.

Sense of Humor

Charles S. Houston, with decades of experience organizing major mountaineering expeditions and research projects at high altitude, looks for humor in expedition participants and says, "The few persons who did not do well did not have a sense of humor."

Without question, the main attribute I look for in selecting participants is a sense of humor. The ability to see the bright side when times get rough may be an asset more valuable than physical conditioning.

Previous Success or Failure

Previous successful or failed participation in wilderness outings has been shown to be a significant predictor.

History of Counseling or Psychological Treatment

An analysis of the medical review process at the National Outdoor Leadership School (NOLS) showed that students who were highly successful tended to be engaged in competitive sports on a regular basis and also had little or no history of counseling or psychological treatment.

I believe there is some validity to the NOLS findings. Having said that, I personally would not exclude anyone who lacked a background of participation in competitive sports and, on a case-by-case basis, I would not categorically reject anyone because he or she had a history of counseling or psychological treatment. I would, however, reject those with a history of serious psychiatric problems.

Leader's Intuition

Psychologic and medical tests may play some role in selecting members for expeditions. Experienced leaders, however, usually place much more confidence in intuition and their personal assessment, derived primarily from the interview, to recognize when a potential expedition member may not work out.

Ultimately, the leader must ask him or herself this one question: "Is this someone I would like to be on a trip with?"

6

UNDERSTANDING YOUR SURROUNDINGS

The Super-Humid Tropical
   Rainforest
The Saturation-Humidity Cloud
   Forest
The Tropical Savanna
The Mangrove Swamp

THE SUPER-HUMID TROPICAL RAINFOREST

The land is one great wild, untidy luxuriant hothouse ...

Charles Darwin

Tropical rainforests, located between the Tropic of Cancer (23°, 27'N latitude) and the Tropic of Capricorn (23°, 27'S latitude), are frost-free regions with at least 4 inches of precipitation per month and a mean annual monthly temperature exceeding 75°F.

Rainforest Peculiarities and Adaptations

As the most biologically diverse community of living things on earth, the tropical rainforest is a realm of superlatives: a *single acre* of tropical forest may contain more than half as many species of trees as occur in *all* the land mass of temperate North America; one square mile of Amazonian forest may be home to double the variety of butterflies that occur in all of the United States and Canada; a single tree in Peru yields as many species of ants as in all of the British Isles . . . well, you get the idea.

The Canopy

Yet another continent of life remains to be discovered, not upon the earth, but one to two hundred feet above it . . .

William Beebe

The relatively recent advent of systematic scientific exploration of the canopy has dramatically changed our view of the rainforest ecosystem: the action is not on the ground, it's high in the sky! Thanks to the development of an ingenious and complicated system of webs, pulleys, and platforms, Donald Perry and others have made it feasible to observe what has been labeled "the most botanically diverse ecosystem on our planet," where two-thirds of the jungle's plants and animals spend their lives.

In addition to observations made directly from treetop platforms, much has been learned about life in the canopy through fogging a marked plot of forest with a powerful insecticide that quickly disperses. After each fogging scientists collect thousands of insect specimens that have fallen from above into nylon trays suspended just above the ground. This technique has made it possible to revise upward the previously accepted estimate of the number of insect species from 10 million to 30 million.

There are many complex but fascinating interrelationships high in the canopy. A common feature of jungle is the abundance of hanging vines called lianas. A heavy load of lianas can be disastrous for trees, causing limbs to break under their weight. From the tree's standpoint this is a *bad thing*. What to do? It appears that jungle trees have evolved to sway out of phase with their neighbors in heavy winds so the vine connections will snap! Not to be terminally stymied, some lianas have managed to maintain their residence in the canopy by growing in a coil-like fashion (not unlike a telephone cord) so that as the trees sway out of sync, the vines simply uncoil and ride out the eviction effort.

Epiphytes—the so-called "air plants"—are found in great profusion attached to limbs and serve to filter out nutrients as rain falls through the multilayers of foliage. In addition to filtering nutrients from rain, epiphytes trap wind-deposited soil and extract minerals, including potassium, phosphorus, and calcium. Some trees have the ability to send aerial roots into the soil mat formed by the epiphytes. These canopy roots provide an efficient mechanism for nutrient recycling.

Rainforest Soils

How is it that nutrient-poor, very old, and highly leached soils of large areas of Amazonia produce such luxuriant forest? In addition to the nutrient-conserving mechanisms at work from the canopy to the tree base, the root system of rainforest trees is extraordinarily efficient at recycling the nutrients from decaying plants to living ones. This recycling system can best be understood through an appreciation of the symbiotic relationship that exists between certain fungi, known collectively as *micorrhizae*, and tree roots.

With your shoe, kick away the leaf litter of the jungle floor and you will encounter the *root mat*, a shallow, tangled mass of tree rootlets interwoven with fungal mycelia. In 1978, Stark and Jordan provided direct evidence showing the extensive root mat itself could take up dissolved nutrients from decomposing organic material or from rainfall and that these nutrients could move directly into the roots *without passing down to the soil*. Tiny rootlets grow up through the soil to attach themselves to leaves that litter the forest floor. Mycorrhizal fungi on the roots send threadlike hyphae into the rotting leaves and, along with associated bacteria, help the tree recover phosphorus, zinc, copper, and other minerals from the forest litter. In addition to helping plants absorb minerals, the fungi may help resist root pathogens. The fungi benefit by taking sugars from the tree.

In addition to the root mat adaptations, *apogeotropic roots* grow vertically upward from the soil onto the stems of neighboring trees. These roots, specially adapted to extremely low soil-nutrient availability in some Amazon forests, absorb and recycle minerals leached from the trees as precipitation flows down the stem. By this nutrient cycling pathway, nutrients are absorbed and transported directly from plant to plant, without entering the soil.

When the forest is disturbed, that is to say when the extensive mat of roots is destroyed, the mechanism for retention of required nutrients is lost. Destruction of the root mat in regions prone to laterization (see below) and continuous cropping on poor soils are key reasons why attempts to establish large-scale agriculture, tree plantations, and permanent pasture have failed in so many areas in the tropics.

If, just a few years ago, you read the scientific literature of soil types occurring in the tropics, you would have come to the conclusion that virtually all of the land, particularly in the Amazon Basin, was unfit for continuous farming and ranching. Today it is recognized that soil types vary regionally in a spectrum of fertility running from extremely poor areas prone to *laterization* (doomed soil that when stripped of vegetation and subjected to heavy rains and heat turns to a bricklike substance) to highly productive tracts occurring in the flood plains or the mineral-rich and easily farmed volcanic soils of, for example, the Andes and Costa Rica.

While it is true that vast areas of tropical soils are nutrient-poor, highly vulnerable to degradation, and unsuited for the usual methods of modern ranching and farming, it is also true that in many areas grazing and farming activities can be carried out if consideration is given to appropriate agricultural practices and site selection. Shuar Indians, who practice slash-and-rot agriculture (fell the trees and let the material rot) on the fertile volcanic soils of the eastern lowlands of Ecuador, maintain same-site crops and pasture land for 20 years and more.

Terra Firme

Terra firme designates rainforest terrain that is sufficiently elevated so it is not subjected to seasonal flooding. Approximately 96 to 97 percent of the Amazonian forest is found completely off the floodplain.

For millennia, indigenous peoples throughout the tropical world have modified their agricultural practices to take advantage of the tendency of lands to return to their original state following human disturbance. Since most of the minerals and nutrients are bound up in the vegetation and not in the soil of terra firme, native inhabitants have adopted the practice of cutting the vegetation from small plots, then setting fire to the vegetation. Through this practice of slash-and-burn agriculture (also known as swidden agriculture), plots are opened up for crop planting and soil is fertilized by the release of minerals and nutrients from the ash. In addition, the alkaline ash makes the soil less acidic. Typically, in slash-and-burn cultivation, crop yield drops annually to the point where plots are usually abandoned within 2 to 3 years. After 14 to 21 years, soil fertility is regenerated by nutrient cycling of forest regrowth and litter. The land may again be cleared and one or two crops may be planted before it is returned again to fallow. Slash-and-burn agriculture is ecologically sound in those areas of the tropics where population density is low.

Várzea

In Amazonia, *várzea* refers to the sediment- and nutrient-rich floodplain forests. Though they make up only a small percentage (approximately 2 percent) of the Amazon Basin, várzea forests are more fertile than their nonflooding and nutrient-poor counterparts; here crops may be planted and harvested year after year without the decline in fertility noted in the terra firme. On the downside, cropping systems in várzea must take into account the high and sometimes unpredictable flood risk.

The notion that cultivation of várzea should have been ideal and widespread among indigenous populations in historical times is supported by the writings of early Europeans who reported large sedentary populations living along the floodplains of Amazonia. Recent assessments that the cost-benefit comparison is not significantly better than with equivalent forms of cultivation on the terra firme, however, have cast doubt on the accuracy of the early European descriptions. Furthermore, there is little *archaeological* evidence that the floodplains invariably supported large native populations in the distant past. Fueling this revisionist assessment is the fact that contemporary indigenous groups largely avoid the várzea and there is little in the way of extensive commercial agriculture practiced along the floodplains today.

THE SATURATION-HUMIDITY CLOUD FOREST

The cloud forest may be thought of as a region between approximately 3,000 to 5,000 feet where there is an almost continuous, dense cloud cover or "mist-belt." It is in the cloud forests of South and Central America and the mossy forests of Southeast Asia that one finds nearly year-round saturation humidity. In certain regions, such as the eastern and western slopes of the Andes in the Republic of Ecuador, cloud forest extends several thousand feet higher than the usually accepted cutoff of 5,000 feet.

Whatever the preponderance of creatures and plants, humans tend to shun areas of cloud forest as a place of permanent residence. On those occasions when I have found myself trekking in cloud forest, or even when passing through on a bus, I have invariably thought, as I anxiously gazed about at the dripping, weird vegetation bathed in a gloomy diffuse light, "I do not belong here." I have seen few structures made by man in cloud forest regions that have a look of permanence or of beauty; houses, animal sheds, and so on have the slapdash appearance of something put up by a tenant discombobulated by nature itself.

THE TROPICAL SAVANNA

Savannas, occurring within the topical zone of Africa and South America, have the appearance of broad, grassy meadows. In South America, seasonal savannas known as *llanos* are found along the floodplain of the Orinoco River throughout southern Venezuela and into parts of Colombia. The vegetation consists of grasses and sedges, and a long, dry season alternates with a rainy season. Trees, if there are any, may appear stunted and are scattered at wide intervals. In the headwaters of the Orinoco River, near the Parima mountain range separating Venezuela and Brazil, discreet patches of savanna occur that are remarkable for their gemlike beauty. The savanna in Africa, extending in a broad belt from western Africa eastward beyond the Nile

River, is dominated by very tall, coarse grasses. Both dwarf and large trees are found in African savanna.

Interestingly, scientists are not in agreement on the causes and conditions that lead to savanna formation or the forces that determine the persistence of savanna ecosystems. It appears that climate, fire, and soil characteristics all play some role in the historical formation of savannas, but the exact role of these forces, as well as the effects of human depredation, are unclear.

THE MANGROVE SWAMP

While not jungle per se, the mangrove swamp deserves some mention if for no other reason than the fact that often one must enter or leave the rainforest by way of the globe-encircling coastal mangrove zone.

The term "mangrove" refers to more than 30 species of salt-tolerant plants that grow along tropical and subtropical tidal coastlines and lagoons. Though botanically unrelated, the trees of the mangrove forest exhibit common morphological adaptations to their saline environment. Mangrove forests best develop 1) under tropical temperatures; 2) near river mouths where abundant soft fertile mud composed of fine silt and clay is available for the growth of seedlings; and 3) on shores free from strong wave action. Such conditions predominate in West Africa, Malaysia, the Pacific Islands, Central and South America, and at the mouth of the Ganges River in India.

Red mangrove (*Rhizophora mangle*), black mangrove (*Avicennia*), and white mangrove (*Laguncularia*) are the three species found in most coastal regions where conditions are suitable for luxuriant mangrove forest. The red mangrove, with its extensive prop-root system and dangling green seed pods, is easily recognized and is found in the intertidal zone. The impressive prop-roots function as supports and also provide oxygen to the below-ground portions of the roots that are buried in anaerobic muds on exposed flats. The seedlings are elongate pods and may reach up to 12 inches in length before dropping from the parent tree. Initially floating horizontally, the seeds are dispersed far and wide by the ocean currents. Eventually, they absorb sufficient water to orient vertically and upon touching suitable substrate, anchor and put out roots. Black mangrove tends to grow in the oxygen-starved sediment that is more shoreward. The black mangrove is immediately identified by the presence of odd-looking breather roots (pneumatophores), which jut out from the mud and supply air transport to the oxygen-starved root system. The sharpness and rigidity of the protruding pneumatophores make walking through black mangrove thickets difficult. White mangrove is less tolerant of prolonged immersion in the sea and grows at slightly higher elevations. Other less salt-tolerant species, including buttonwood (*Conocarpus*), grow at still higher elevations back from areas subject to tidal flooding.

A word of caution regarding approaching mangrove shores by boat: from the sea, typical mangrove islands are extremely hard to tell apart; one island looks like another. Unless made conspicuous by reliable navigation markers (seldom found in developing nations), the myriad channels that exist in low-lying mangrove regions are nearly impossible to navigate accurately without a local pilot.

The mangrove swamp as a source of food is discussed in Chapter 15.

THRIVING ON THE TRAIL

COPING WITH THE JUNGLE ENVIRONMENT
Living with the Wetness
Coping with Heat and Humidity
Sun Exposure

JUNGLE TREKKING
Choosing a Guide/Porter
Trekking Tips
Duration of Jungle Travel and Emotional
      Response
Patterns

CAMP LIFE
Shelter
Food
Potable Water

HAZARDS (REAL AND IMAGINED)
Arthropods
Fish
Amphibians
Mammals
Reptiles
Plants

7

COPING WITH THE JUNGLE ENVIRONMENT

Living with Wetness
Coping with Heat and Humidity
Sun Exposure

A visit to the rainforests of the New World tropics can be either a sublime experience or a hellish ordeal.

Adrian Forsyth and Ken Miyata

The super-humid, lowland rainforest gets up to 450 inches of rain a year; by contrast the State of Indiana averages about 40 inches a year. In the higher-elevation cloud forest there is a continuous, dense cloud cover throughout the year accompanied by a constant mist or drizzle. In such settings of heat and high humidity, people become mentally fatigued as a result of being constantly wet. At some point it occurs to most people who spend a lot of time in the jungle, particularly during the rainy season, that they will never be dry again . . . ever!

In this chapter you will learn critical coping skills that should help you deal with the jungle . . . before it deals with you.

LIVING WITH WETNESS

Fortunately, travelers can be perfectly content during even long stays in the tropics if they employ basic strategies for coping with the physical and psychological burden of wetness. There are three fundamentals of living with wetness:

- *Revelation No. 1:* Wetness is as much a state of mind as it is a physical condition.

- *Revelation No. 2:* It's okay to be wet!

- *Revelation No. 3:* Your body, particularly your feet, must be dry in camp and at night.

Newcomers to the tropics commonly waste inordinate energy in behaviors designed to avoid getting wet; experienced jungle hands stride right on through streams and puddles without skipping a beat. I spent my first few trips to tropical rainforests trying to avoid swamps and mud puddles, attempting—unsuccessfully—to stay dry during the frequent rains. The day I stopped trying to stay dry on the trail was the day I truly began to fully enjoy the jungle experience. I know this sounds too simple to be true, but taking to heart my three "revelations" is your shortcut to contentment.

Dryness while trekking or working during the daylight hours is not a requisite for physical or mental health. Wetness does not equate with illness, significant discomfort, or dampened spirits. People can tolerate being wet throughout much of the day if they know for certain that they have a dry change of clothes and dry boots to wear in camp and that they will be dry at night. In addition to the psychological benefits, being dry at night means that maceration (skin softening and erosion) is less likely to develop where two areas of skin are in contact—for example, breasts or groin.

Bedding and clothing can be protected from moisture by careful wrapping in plastic garbage bags. Despite all efforts, however, eventually certain "dry" items become damp or accidentally soaked. In such instances the wet articles should be spread out on shrubs and bushes. They will dry within 2 hours in full sun in the tropics. In sub-Saharan Africa, myiasis (maggot infestation) due to the tumbu fly, *Cordylobia anthropophaga*, can be avoided by hanging clothing to dry in bright sunlight, never on the ground. Cloth dried over a wood fire tends to pick up unpleasant odors that repeated washing will not remove.

COPING WITH HEAT AND HUMIDITY

Your Response to Heat and Humidity

For all practical purposes, humans have no physiological ability to acclimatize to a cold environment. Eskimos, arctic explorers, and mountaineers are able to survive at extremes of cold because of the protection offered by layering of clothing. Fortunately, humans do have an ability to acclimatize physiologically to a hot environment. Mechanisms of human adaptation to heat include the initiation of sweating at a lower core temperature, doubling of sweating, various cardiovascular changes, and a marked increase in metabolic efficiency.

Radiation and evaporation are the mechanisms that account for most of the heat dissipating from the body. Radiation, the transfer of heat from the body to a cooler environment, accounts for approximately 65 percent of cooling as long as the air temperature is lower than body temperature. High temperature blocks radiation; when ambient temperature approaches 95°F., evaporation is the only mechanism the body has to significantly dissipate heat. Approximately 30 percent of cooling results from the evaporation of sweat. High humidity blocks evaporation. *Sweat that drips from the skin exacerbates dehydration without providing any cooling benefit.*

Predisposing Factors to Heat Illness

Certain factors predispose individuals to develop heat problems:

Advanced Age Elderly individuals are often dehydrated to begin with and are less able to increase cardiac output for heat dissipation.

Extreme Youth Babies and small children lack thermoregulatory mechanisms for sufficient sweating.

Obesity Obese individuals don't have sufficient surface area to dissipate the heat their volume generates.

Patients with Hyperthyroidism These individuals have an increased metabolic rate with increased endogenous heat production.

Patients Taking Medications Patients taking beta-blockers, ACE inhibitors, diuretics, and anticholinergics are at increased risk of developing heat problems. Those who take amphetamines, PCP, cocaine, and LSD are at greater risk.

Preventing Heat Illness

Acclimatize Before undertaking long-distance trekking in the tropics, acclimatize by spending *at least 4 days* in a hot, humid environment and engaging in *moderate daily exercise* there. Just hanging out in a hot and humid environment will not lead to rapid acclimatization; you must exercise and sweat to get the desired effect. This acclimatization will be lost within a week if not maintained.

Maintain Adequate Hydration Dehydration interferes with the process of heat acclimation that puts you at risk for heat exhaustion and heat stroke. The following schedule satisfactorily maintains hydration during the strenuous exercise of jungle trekking:

- Before setting off on the trail, drink a liter/quart of disinfected water.

- A half hour later drink a second liter.

- One hour after the second liter, drink a third, then consume approximately 1 liter every 2 to 4 hours throughout the day while on the trail.

Get in the habit of drinking water on the schedule just outlined, and do *not* rely on thirst as an indicator of the need to replace fluids. By the time you have a craving for liquids, significant losses may have occurred. By the same token, quenching thirst does not mean you have adequately replaced lost fluid.

Oral Rehydration Salts   Oral rehydration salts (ORS) come in premeasured packets that, when added to a liter of disinfected water, provide an ideal balance for replacing lost electrolytes. It is a good idea to put rehydration salts into the first liter of water you drink before setting out on the trail. After especially strenuous days, drink a second liter with them in the evening. ORS packets are distributed throughout the developing world by the World Health Organization and UNICEF, but they are hard to come by in the commercial market overseas. In the United States, oral rehydration therapy packets may be obtained from Cera Products (888–237–2598), and Jianas Brothers (816–241–2880), or from recreational use suppliers such as Chinook Medical Gear, Inc. (*www. chinookmed.com*). Sports mixtures such as Gatorade are tasty and will to some degree maintain adequate electrolyte balance, but not nearly as well as ORS. Salt *tablets* are *not* recommended because they are gastric irritants and may actually delay acclimatization.

Proper Clothing   Wear ultra-lightweight, light-colored, and loose-fitting cotton clothing and a wide-brimmed hat.

Travel Light   Travel light (see Chapter 3) and, whenever possible, have a native porter carry *all* gear.

During 35 years of jungle trekking, traveling solo (just myself and Indian companions) or with sizeable groups of North Americans and Europeans, I have not seen anyone become significantly dehydrated or develop life-threatening, heat-related illness, *if they followed the preceding recommendations.*

Muscle Cramps

A few years ago, a slightly overweight, otherwise fit 30-year-old man accompanied me on a fast dash to check out some odd geologic features I had encountered during a previous trek in the Siapa River region of southern Venezuela. We started our hike at 11:00 A.M. and, maintaining a fairly brisk pace, arrived at our destination by 1:30 P.M. Along the way, we each consumed approximately 3 quarts of iodine-treated water. I, fortunately, mixed a packet of ORS in my first quart of water; my friend did not.

After spending an hour or so at the site, we each consumed a quart of water, and began the return journey to camp. Two hours into the return leg, it became apparent that my friend was feeling somewhat fatigued, but he soldiered on. After another 15 minutes, I noticed that he was sweating profusely and called a halt to rest for a spell. During the rest stop, he consumed an additional two quarts of iodine-treated water.

When we reached camp, he immediately downed a quart of purified water. While sitting on a block of wood, he suddenly seized his right calf and began massaging it. "Damn, muscle cramp!" Within 5 minutes, the other calf went into spasm. As he was massaging his calves, he cried out and fell back onto the ground, writhing in pain. Both thighs were simultaneously in maximal spasm and were, literally, boardlike in their rigidity.

Cause of Muscle Cramps Muscle cramps of the calves commonly occur after prolonged periods of vigorous exercise. Severe contractions of the thigh muscles, a rare event, usually occur within minutes to an hour after cessation of strenuous hiking when large amounts of water are ingested without adequate salt replacement. The exquisitely painful, tetanic contractions of these large, powerful muscles are truly frightening to the victim (and onlookers!).

Treatment Immediate treatment of cramps includes gentle movement, massage, and stretching of the affected muscles. The individual administering first aid should, in a calm voice, frequently reassure the victim that the ordeal will soon be over. Spasms may stop and start again in a series of recurrences over a period of a quarter to half hour, and ORS should be given.

Prevention To eliminate or reduce the chances of intensely painful leg cramps rousing you from sleep, *always* perform calf-stretching exercises before hitting the trail each morning and, especially, at night before falling asleep. From personal experience, I can tell you that there are few things in life more unpleasant and alarming than being awakened from a deep sleep by spasms of the calf muscles; avoid the problem by taking the few extra minutes to stretch!

Severe daytime calf and thigh spasms can be prevented by maintaining hydration, using ORS, and performing stretching exercises before and after demanding physical exertion.

Heat Swelling

Swelling (edema) of the lower legs and ankles often develops in otherwise healthy individuals during the first week of travel in hot environments. This condition is self-limited and does not require medical therapy. Keeping the legs elevated, when possible, will help reduce the swelling.

The fingers may swell rapidly and dramatically with vigorous activity in the hot, humid rainforest. To avoid the need for emergency ring removal, take off all rings prior to jungle trekking.

Skin Problems

Intertrigo Intertrigo (maceration), a softening and erosion of the skin where two areas of skin are in contact, occurs commonly in hot, humid environments. Male trekkers often have problems where the skin of the scrotum (or underwear) rubs against the inner thigh. This condition is usually corrected by applying a thin layer of Bactroban ointment to the affected area morning and night for several days. Women may develop a rash from *Candida* (a common skin yeast) underneath the breasts and can get relief by using Lotrisone cream.

Heat Rash Common heat rash, also known as "prickly heat" or *miliaria* (not to be confused with *malaria!*), is caused by blockage of the sweat duct openings. The diagnosis is easy: the sufferer has recently been exposed to excessive heat and humidity and is covered by hundreds of small bumps that itch and burn. The distribution of the eruption is predominantly on the neck, back, chest, sides of the trunk, abdomen, and skin folds. The condition responds to cooling and drying affected skin and taking Benadryl or another antihistamine to relieve itching.

To prevent many common forms of skin problems in the tropics, do what native tribesmen do: take a bath in a nearby stream every evening.

Heat Exhaustion

The combination of high temperature and high humidity found in the tropical rainforest blocks the two main mechanisms the body has to dissipate heat. This places the traveler at risk for heat exhaustion and, further along the continuum of serious heat-related illness, heat stroke.

Heat exhaustion is characterized by flulike symptoms, which may include nausea, vomiting, diarrhea, malaise, headache, dizziness, and muscle cramps. In addition, there may be a rapid, weak pulse and minor confusion. The temperature may be normal or slightly elevated. Do *not* rely on the presence or absence of sweating to make the diagnosis.

When heat exhaustion is suspected, move the patient to a cool, shaded environment and remove all restrictive clothing. Wet down the victim and fan him to promote evaporation and cooling. Jungle streams in hilly or mountainous regions may be surprisingly cool; soaking the victim in one of these streams may help. If ice or ice packs are available, place them where the blood supply is nearest the skin surface: on the neck, in the armpits and groin, and against the chest wall. Administer ORS. Do *not* use alcohol to sponge the victim. Do *not* give aspirin or acetaminophen.

Heat Stroke

Heat exhaustion is serious enough—heat stroke can be deadly: approximately 80 percent of victims of heat stroke die if not treated promptly and effectively. Heat exhaustion must not be allowed to progress to heat stroke.

Here are the main clues to diagnosing heat stroke:

1. *Elevated core body temperature.* Heat stroke is imminent when the core (rectal) temperature approaches 41°C (approximately 106°F). Core body temperature is determined with a rectal thermometer, not from a thermometer reading under the tongue or in the armpit. Do not make a judgment based on whether the patient *feels* hot; although most victims will feel warm or hot to the touch, some do not.

2. *Ataxia* (loss of coordination, staggering). The cerebellum, the part of the nervous system that deals with coordination, is very sensitive to heat.

3. *Confusion.* Patients with impending heat stroke become confused and exhibit bizarre behavior. Eventually the victim may develop seizures, become comatose, and die.

4. *Rapid breathing.*

5. *Rapid heart rate.* Although the heart is beating faster than usual, the blood pressure is lower than normal.

Impending heat stroke should be considered in the patient who exhibits signs of heat exhaustion and also develops confusion, odd behavior, and staggers when attempting to walk in a straight line. *Sweating may be present or absent* in heat stroke and, contrary to popular belief, must not be used as a criterion for diagnosis!

Heat stroke is a true medical emergency and carries a significant risk of death even with appropriate treatment. *Begin cooling immediately:* the more rapid the cooling, the lower the morbidity and mortality. As in the case of heat exhaustion: if ice or cold packs are available, place them on the neck, armpits, and groin; wet the victim down with water and fan vigorously; immerse the victim in a cool stream if available. Do not give anything by mouth because of the risk of vomiting and aspiration. If possible, immediately transport the victim to the nearest medical facility for more definitive treatment.

Constipation

The last thing most participants on jungle outings in third-world settings expect to be bothered with is constipation. A combination of mild dehydration and "trail" food creates perfect conditions for the development of bowel sluggishness and hardened feces. As Paul Auerbach notes, "The city backpacker diet of chocolate bars, peanuts, and cheese sandwiches will turn the most irascible bowels into mortar."

Constipation can be avoided by drinking fluids often and in quantity and adding fiber to the diet in the form of vegetables and fruit. It is a good idea to have on hand a stool softener such as Colace or a bulking agent such as Metamucil to help prevent constipation or to get things moving again.

SUN EXPOSURE

Damage from the Sun

Overexposure to sun and the damage caused by ultraviolet radiation (UVR) can lead to sunburn, aging of the skin, and skin cancer. Except along open areas of river and large clearings, sunburn is not a major concern when traveling through the tropical forest, because the canopy assures adequate protection from the sun's harmful rays. I often return from long trips in the jungle more pale than when I started the journey.

Physicians divide skin types into six distinct classes:

- Type I   Always burns, never tans.
- Type II   Easily burns, rarely tans.
- Type III   Sometimes burns, usually tans.
- Type IV   Rarely burns, always tans.
- Type V   Tans profusely.
- Type VI   Never (or almost never) burns.

Obviously, those who fall into Types I, II, and III have special need to protect their skin from the sun's rays. Tanning, sunburn, and more serious damage to the skin are caused by UVR light, which includes wavelengths between 200 and 400 nanometers (nm).

Ultraviolet C (UVC)

UVC (200–280 nm) is of little concern at present in that it is absorbed by the ozone and upper atmosphere and doesn't reach earth. Human exposure to UVC generally comes about through germicidal lamps and acetylene torches.

Ultraviolet B (UVB)

UVB (280–320 nm) is the major cause of sunburn. UVB also contributes to chronic skin injury, skin aging, and skin cancer.

Ultraviolet A (UVA)

UVA (320–400 nm) causes most photosensitivity reactions. UVA also contributes to chronic skin damage, causes sunburn, and is a co-carcinogen with UVB. Sun parlors utilize high-output UVA and are not safe.

Several factors influence the intensity and exposure to UVR. For example, the time of day is quite significant. The maximum intensity occurs when the sun is directly overhead. In southern California, 15 minutes' exposure at noon is equivalent to 3 hours' exposure at 5 P.M. The season is obviously significant in northern latitudes, but in the tropics the calender month is of little relevance. Finally, altitude is a very important determinant of UVR exposure. For each 1,000-foot increase in elevation above sea level, there is a 4 percent increase in UVB exposure. Thus, climbers and backpackers at 10,000 feet have 40 percent more exposure at midday than someone at the same latitude at sea level.

Various drugs may sensitize the skin to the sun's harmful rays. Drugs commonly incriminated include tetracycline, nonsteroidal anti-inflammatory drugs, Retin-A, Accutane, and thiazide diuretics.

Protection from the Sun

Always wear lightweight, long-sleeved shirts when exposed to prolonged periods in the sun. A wide-brim hat, which can be wadded up for travel, is excellent for sun protection.

Sunscreens are thought to offer considerable protection from UVR. Although all sunscreens block UVB to some degree, certain sunscreens offer superior protection in that they block more UVB and partially block UVA.

Which screen is best? First, you need to know how sunscreens are rated. All sunscreens sold today carry the SPF (Sun Protection Factor) rating. SPF is determined by taking the minimal erythema dose (MED)—the exposure time to produce the barest erythema (abnormal redness of the skin) of sun-protected skin—and dividing it by the MED of nonprotected skin:

$$SPF = \frac{MED \text{ of Protected Skin}}{MED \text{ of Unprotected Skin}}$$

As an example, a product rated SPF 15 requires 15 times the amount of exposure to produce minimal erythema compared to using no sunscreen. In actual practice, anything above SPF 15 is probably irrelevant as far as protection goes. Because travel in the tropics often involves water immersion and sweating, a "waterproof" or "water-resistant" sunscreen should be chosen. To be fully effective, sunscreens should be applied about 30 minutes before exposure to the sun to allow penetration into skin.

An important and often misunderstood point is this: if your skin will develop minimal erythema without protection in one hour, a product with an SPF of 4 will provide only 4 hours of protection *no matter how many times it is applied.* That is to say, one does not get 4 more hours of protection after each application!

Because a significant percentage of individuals develop a rash or burning and stinging around the eyes when using products containing PABA, it is best to purchase a sunscreen that is labeled "hypoallergenic" and "PABA free."

Opaque formulations containing zinc oxide, titanium dioxide, or talc prevent all solar radiation from reaching the skin and are excellent for the nose, lips, and the tips of the ears. Family Practice resident physicians and medical school students who accompany me to the tropics seem to delight in painting themselves up "Indian" fashion with the wild colors available in these products.

8

JUNGLE TREKKING

Choosing a Guide/Porter
Trekking Tips
Duration of Jungle Travel and
Emotional Response Patterns

For the following discussion on jungle trekking, two assumptions have been made: 1) you are doing serious, long-distance trekking (and not just ambling down a National Park trail with signs posted as navigation aids); and 2) you are accompanied by a knowledgeable guide. See Chapter 15 for recommendations about what to do if you are traversing unknown jungle without an escort.

CHOOSING A GUIDE/PORTER

There is one overarching rule for jungle travel: *you must always be accompanied by a knowledgeable guide.* Even after 80 trips into the jungles of Central and South America, I would never consider going it alone or setting off without someone who was jungle-reared. Indigenous tribesmen will not get lost and can always find food and water. Using readily available plant materials they can quickly and expertly fashion tools, weapons, and shelter. Engaging the services of a native guide is the best insurance policy you can have.

Occasionally travelers are left behind on the trail by indigenous guides. Unintentional desertion happens when trekkers hire natives who have had no previous experience with neophytes. Realizing almost at once that their charges cannot keep up on the trail, the natives run ahead and sit down to rest, not knowing that others cannot navigate the trail alone. Travelers who want to avoid being left behind on the trail should hire a guide who is experienced in traveling with nonnatives.

I happen to trek in extremely isolated regions of Amazonia where potential Indian guides often have had no experience with outsiders and often have never before seen any human who is not a member of their own linguistic tribal group. Under these circumstances, I make it clear (through an interpreter if need be) that at no time am I to be beyond the range of sight or voice contact with the guide or porter. In this fashion I travel for weeks at a time. What to do if you do get left behind on the trail? Stay put! Someone eventually will return to find you.

Depending on the circumstances, suitable guides and porters can usually be identified with the help of the village headman, local schoolteacher, village health worker, missionaries, and anthropologists. Beware the teenage guide/porter! These fellows are so bursting with energy they have genuine difficulty slowing down to any pace that you can maintain. I'm convinced these supremely fit young men find it physically uncomfortable and psychologically stressful to maintain a slower pace.

There is always the issue of payment for the services of a guide/porter. In the truly remote regions where I trek, more often than not my assistants are outside the money economy. In such a setting, I find trade-goods, such as spools of monofilament fish line (40- to 100-pound test for big fish in big rivers; 10-pound test for smaller fish), fish hooks, machetes, and axes are more desirable than cash. In regions where the locals have had significant contact with the outside world, cash, or a combination of cash and trade-goods, will be expected.

TREKKING TIPS

Using a Machete

As I've already mentioned, a machete is the single most essential tool for jungle survival and for the many tasks in camp and on the trail that require steel with a sharp edge. A proper machete (long, heavy, and well made) in experienced hands is worth its weight in gold. Also, machetes make excellent gifts and are often more desirable than cash for payment of services.

The machete is not used to hack at the foliage in a frenzy. In the hands of an expert, the finely honed machete is swung with rhythm and grace; cuts are made sparingly and selectively with near-surgical precision.

Machetes are dangerous tools. It is especially hazardous to use a machete in the rain or when cutting wet grass; the weapon may fly right out of the hand. Also, when cutting brush, the worker often encounters sawgrass. The resulting skin lacerations, which are not noticed at first because sawgrass is razor-sharp, may take a week or two to heal. Because of the risks involved, an experienced individual should be in charge of transporting and using the machete.

March in File

It is important to follow a particular order on the trail: put a guide in front to identify the proper course and—no small thing—dispatch snakes. You follow behind; put your porter(s) to the rear. Never bring up the rear! (Unless, of course, you are traveling with just one native serving as guide/porter.)

Tooling Down the Trail

Indigenous peoples move along the trail at a rapid, sustained pace, somewhere at the upper end of fast walking and just before breaking into a run. They seldom slow down for any reason, but they will speed up when fleeing enemies, pursuing game, or hurrying home to sleep in their own hammock or bed at night. Not only do they move along at this clip on level ground and downhill, but they also keep the same pace going uphill! Chances are, you do not maintain your regular pace when ascending an incline, and initially you will find this trait among natives perplexing and tiring. Tribesmen know what they are doing here . . . their idea is to maintain a constant rate as they move from point A to point B, and it doesn't occur to them that going up a hill is any more reason to go at a slower pace than when walking on level ground. Remember, they are supremely fit, so going uphill really isn't all that much more taxing than walking on level ground. By the same token, they do not go faster when going downhill. It's just a steady and, for them, comfortable gait. Back home, as you are getting in shape (physically and mentally) for jungle trekking, you should hike at a fast pace and practice maintaining your speed regardless of the terrain.

Stride

You will notice something else besides the speed natives maintain on the trail: they move with a graceful stride. Like anyone who is good at what they do, there is no wasted motion. Once in the jungle, try to imitate their energy-saving, fluid rhythm.

When You Fall

I exhausted myself trying to remain upright, it was futile. Of the first few days in the jungle I remember the muddy slopes and river rocks coming up to meet my face with astonishing regularity.

Eric Hansen

Fall you must. Inattention, an unexpected slick spot on the trail, exhaustion, or just plain bad luck will eventually reacquaint you with the force of gravity and down you will go. Unless a fall would almost certainly lead to serious injury or death—a rare situation—you must overcome the instinct to grab the first thing handy. Spine-bearing plants, often growing exactly where you reflexively reach out for support, are an ever-present hazard in many jungle regions—especially in Central and South America. A puncture wound in a joint space of the hand can lead to impressive complications. (See "Armed or Spine-Bearing Plants" in the section on thriving on the trail.) It seems counterintuitive, but as often as not, it is best to simply take the fall and pick yourself up with little more damage than slight embarrassment. I often take neophyte trekkers out into the jungle, find a relatively safe muddy slope and make everyone purposefully practice crumpling to the ground.

Rehearsing what to do when you fall allows you to consciously override the urge to grab when it happens for real on the trail. (I have fallen so many times over the years, I don't have to practice!)

Getting the Hang of It

It is amazing how well your body and mind will adapt to trail conditions. No, you will probably never be as good as the least adept native in the entire Amazon Basin when it comes to trail performance, but you will gain a surprising degree of ability and confidence in a relatively short time.

The reality of heightened performance was brought home to me once when traveling with a small band of Indians in southern Venezuela. We were on an expedition to collect arrow-grass in the vicinity of an abandoned village 2 hard days' trek away from our home village. My companions were a bit edgy during much of the trip because we were passing through the territory of a neighboring tribe with whom they were at war; in a raid the previous year several villagers had been killed. To complicate matters, armed *garimpeiros* (Brazilian gold miners) were active in the region.

On the last day of the return leg, as daylight faded, it became apparent the Indians had decided to press on and arrive back at our home base sometime during the night. We were traveling in deep forest which, even in daylight hours, had a gloomy aspect due to the dense canopy overhead. Two hours after true sunset, on a night with no moon and all starlight blocked by a full cloud cover, I found myself bounding down the trail at a rate somewhere between a trot and a full run with Indians who absolutely refused to slow down or stop. I realized I had no choice but to keep up.

Though aware that I could break a bone or be knocked unconscious from tripping over the rocks and roots beneath my feet and that my eyes were endangered by unseen branches and needle-sharp spines, I kept up the pace, driven in part by the shared anxiety of potential harm from the *garimpeiros* and nearby hostile Indians. I can only assume that, in this state of hyper-alertness, my senses were working overtime to subliminally process every conceivable visual, tactile, auditory, and olfactory cue.

Now the curious part: at some point, I entered a mysterious zone of performance where I had the distinct sensation that the trail irregularities and hazards had vanished. My feet seemed to glide over the terrain and I found myself effortlessly dodging hazards as they registered somewhere below the threshold of consciousness: a joining of physical and spiritual realms that I can only liken to the feeling one has of sailing on a calm sea when fair winds carry your vessel over the water as though in a dream. I have not had this ultimate sense of exhilaration before or since. It is, I suspect, an experience tribesmen have every time they travel through the tropical forest, and I wouldn't be surprised to learn that elite athletes share the same enigmatic high on a regular basis.

DURATION OF JUNGLE TRAVEL AND EMOTIONAL RESPONSE PATTERNS

Research has shown that mood states of participants in wilderness outings fluctuate in a fairly predictable pattern. Because of an almost inevitable deterioration in the health of expeditioners after 2 to 3 weeks of trekking in remote areas, many experienced group leaders limit expeditions to no more than 3 weeks. See Chapter 5 for additional insights into predictable emotional response patterns of expedition participants over time and recommendations for handling deteriorating group interactions.

Coping with Unexpected Delays

As they succeeded one another, each day seemed longer than the one before; waiting became obsessive and impotent inactivity a full-time occupation.

Tony Parker, *Lighthouse*

Sometimes travelers face unexpected delays in the jungle. Various factors contribute to this state of affairs, such as inclement weather, mechanical problems with aircraft, or political turmoil that shuts down public transportation. Many people stuck in a remote locale respond with anger and irritability. This attitude certainly does not improve the situation and can be devastating in the context of group dynamics. It is far better to accept the situation and use the additional time to appreciate the aesthetic qualities of the tropical forest. Unhurried strolls along a jungle path reveal small and captivating discoveries. Photography can help keep the spirits high and foster creativity.

It helps to shift out of gear mentally and allow the intellectual machinery to idle. Nearly everyone has had the experience of driving for hours and arriving at a destination with virtually no recollection of anything. The same thing can be accomplished in the village setting by just lying around in a hammock. The hours and days pass surprisingly quickly. This experience is akin to cruising in a sailboat with no engine . . . the person learns patience and develops an appreciation that the rhythms of nature are not governed by the ticking of a clock. For many visitors to the jungle, unexpected isolation opens up a new world as they come to experience the biospheric cadence.

9

CAMP LIFE

Shelter
Food
Potable Water

SHELTER

Existing Dwellings

Natives rarely spend the night in makeshift shelters, and even then only because of absolute necessity. With few exceptions it is best to use existing dwellings for slinging a hammock or putting down a sleeping pad.

Common courtesy governs the placement of a hammock or sleeping pad inside the hut of a native. Certain spots are used throughout the day or night for domestic duties. Also, there are often places in huts where no one ever sits or sleeps or where only men or women are permitted out of custom. Since travelers will not know where such taboo spots are, they should ask before bedding down.

Tarp

Under circumstances where huts are not available for use, a properly rigged tarpaulin provides satisfactory shelter from the rain. Rip-stop polyethylene tarps (8 × 10 feet) are lightweight and waterproof. Coated nylon tarps are also acceptable but must be sealed with a product such as Seam Grip.

Here's a typical method of erecting a tarp. First, a fairly stout line is run between two trees at a height of 7 to 8 feet off the ground and is cinched tight. Second, the long axis of the tarp is centered over this rope, and ropes attached to the middle grommets on each end are tied to the trees. Third, the corner grommets are tied to whatever trees, bushes, or strong clumps of grass are handy. In addition to the corner tie-downs, a tie-down in the middle on each side is helpful. The sides of the roof should be made high enough to enter and exit conveniently, yet not so high that driving rain can come in at an angle.

Never assume that just because the stars are twinkling brightly in a clear sky means the conditions will stay that way for long. In minutes, clouds can move in and shed rain that falls hard enough to shake the earth. A person who has not prepared shelter thoughtfully and well will pay the consequences.

Slinging a Hammock

Once the tarp is up, the hammock ropes are run through the sleeves of the mosquito net. Then the hammock is slung. It takes practice to get a hammock slung just right. The basic idea is to have a certain curve to the hammock that is proportioned for comfort. Also, the hammock should be suspended high enough that it will not sag to the ground during the night as it naturally gives under an adult's weight, yet not so high off the ground that falling out of the hammock will lead to injury. Practice slinging your hammock at home without a mosquito net: choose varying heights where the rope ends are tied to vertical or horizontal supports and learn how to adjust for short or long distances between supports. While you are at it, you might as well spend a few nights sleeping in a hammock at home—that's the surest way to satisfy yourself you have mastered the art of slinging a hammock.

Mosquito Net

Next the mosquito net is suspended. The ropes running from tree to tarp, from tree to mosquito net, and from tree to hammock should be sprayed with DEET insect repellent to keep ants and other pests from using the ropes as trails. Finally, a few broad leaves (banana leaves or heliconia are perfect) are folded down at the spine and one or two are draped over the bare rope extending from the tree to the tarp, allowing the leaf nearest the tarp to "shingle" onto the tarp. This keeps rain from running down the tarp and hammock ropes.

Knots

Knowledge of two knots is needed for slinging a hammock. These knots always hold and always come undone quickly without jamming.

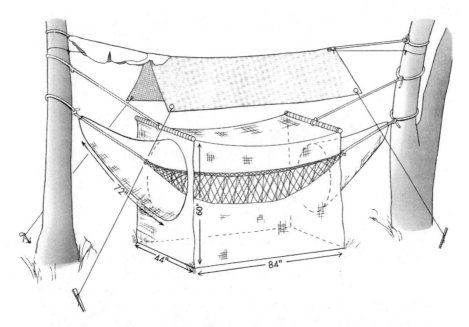

Construction of mosquito netting for use with a hammock: sleeve hole = 88 inches in circumference; small hole = 18 inches in circumference; smallest holes (for supporting sticks) = 4 inches in circumference.

The *half hitch* is used to tie the hammock to a horizontal beam.

1. Pass the working end of the rope around the object to which it is to be secured.

2. Pass the working end of the rope around again without crossing over itself.

3. Bring the end over and around the standing part and through the loop that has just been created. You have just made a half hitch.

4. Make a second half hitch below the first half hitch.

5. Pull tight.

The *camel hitch* is used to tie the hammock to a vertical post so securely that the user can sleep soundly knowing the knot will stay exactly where it was tied:

1. Make three turns downward around the vertical pole.

2. Bring the working end up and over the turns.

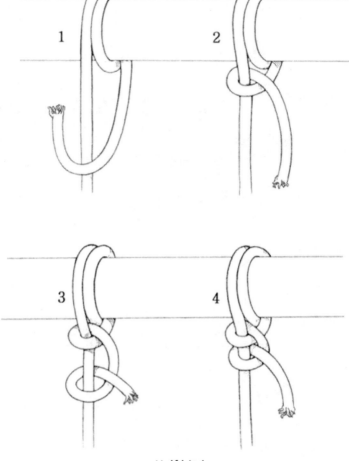

Half hitch

3. Make a turn at the top and pass the end back under itself.

4. Make a second turn at the top and pass the end back under itself.

Tent

The use of a tent as shelter in the tropical rainforest is *not* recommended. Clearing a tent space is time consuming, and the stumps remaining from cutting saplings and bushes invariably perforate the floor. Air does not circulate; after a restless night sweltering in the tent the traveler emerges tired, sticky, and irritable.

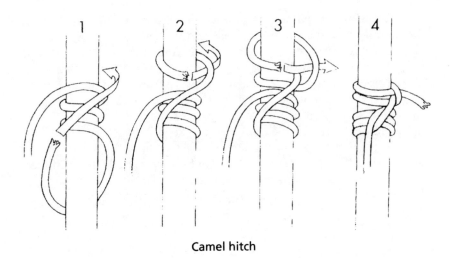

Camel hitch

FOOD

I get the hands of one of the monkeys. . . . This is the choice morsel reserved for guests whom one wishes to honor, so I am obliged to suck up these sad fingers with a show of conviction befitting a well-mannered guest.

Philippe Descola

Solitary travelers or small groups usually do not need to carry in large amounts of food. Edibles are always available in areas inhabited by friendly natives; the locals must be eating something.

Animals

Travelers in the tropics must be open to eating the food that is available locally. Most creatures, whether they walk, crawl, slither, hop, scuttle, swim, or fly, are good to eat. So, persons confronted with boiled caiman (alligator), cooked capybara (a 50-kg rodent), or a plate of roasted palm grubs (larvae of *Rhynchophorus* spp.) should eat and be glad for food on the table. Raw palm grubs, which grow up to 5 inches long, are quite tasty and are a great favorite of Amazonian Indians. They are eaten by slashing open the thin integument with the thumbnail, extracting and discarding the intestinal tract, placing the opened skin to the mouth, and sucking out the turgid contents. Like so many unpleasant-looking edible things (the oyster comes to mind), the palm grub is a great delicacy.

In addition to palm grubs, more than 20 species of edible insects, including ants and termites, are collected year-round by the people of Amazonia. Insects are a source of energy, animal protein, and fat, and they function to add diversity to the diet. Large (10-inch diameter!) hairy spiders, *Theraphosa leblondi*, are often captured and roasted on an open fire. After the barbed hairs are singed off, the spider is placed in the embers away from the hottest part of the fire. Prepared in this manner, spiders have a pleasant, shrimplike taste.

Indians of the Americas have perfected the art of smoking fish and meat so that they remain safe to eat for long periods. It is common to see huge hunks of tapir meat or monstrous slabs of 100-pound catfish resting on racks, coal black from the smoking process.

Plants

The tropics have an abundance of flora as food. The yard-long heart of palm is cool and delicious when eaten in its raw state or may be included in a soup spiced with tropical herbs. Several tropical fruits that make their way to grocers in North America and Europe should be familiar to the traveler: the papaya, excellent with a layering of lime juice; the mango, pungent but superb; and the juicy, sweet pineapple. In recent years consumers outside the tropics have experienced the delights of the passion fruit (*Passiflora* spp.) in fruit-based drinks. There are numerous New World fruits that often have no name in English and generally have not found their way into the world market: chirimoya, guanabana, pitahayas, naranjilla, uchuva, tamarillo, zapote, sapotilla, and bade, to name a few. The boiled fruit of the peach palm, *Bactries gasipaes*, is nutritious and flavorful.

The banana and its cousin, the plantain, provide a large percentage of the total caloric intake of natives in the American and African tropics. Curiously, in many native villages it is difficult to find the sweet, finger-length bananas and the common yellow bananas that are exported by the billions from tropical countries. It is, alas, the green plantain that features prominently in the daily fare of inhabitants of the tropics. The plantain cannot be faulted because of any disagreeable taste, since it has little taste at all. It is the fruit's exceptional dryness that makes it so unpalatable. Indeed, the most hardened tropical traveler may emit an audible groan when served a plate of dry, roasted plantains.

Yucca (manioc or cassava), *Manihot esculenta*, is a staple source of carbohydrate nutrition throughout the Americas and much of tropical Africa. There are two kinds of yucca: the "sweet" and the "bitter." They are both the same species but differ in the distribution and amount of a poisonous constituent, a cyanogenic glycoside, in the root. To the eye, sweet and bitter yucca cannot be easily distinguished; one must know which variety was planted. Sweet yucca, commonly encountered in the eastern lowlands of the Andean countries of Colombia, Ecuador, and Peru, is eaten after the bark containing the toxic substance is peeled off and the root is boiled. In bitter yucca, the poison is more concentrated and distributed throughout the root, so it must be extracted before consumption. Amerindians have devised an ingenious apparatus, the *tipití,* that expresses the poisonous juice from the peeled and grated flour of the manioc roots.

Prepackaged Food

Travelers in a large group should carry dried, packaged foods, since the host village might not be able to provide sufficient foodstuffs or they might pass through truly isolated or unexplored regions that are uninhabited. Packaged foods should be carried by travelers in regions where the locals are known to be inhospitable.

Dried instant food simply needs the addition of water to make a good and hearty meal. A few selections should be tried before a large supply for field use is ordered. It is not necessary to add hot water to all packaged foods; adding purified, ambient-temperature water produces acceptable results for most foods. Drawbacks to prepackaged foods include the expense, the space they take up, and the matter of dealing with the empty foil packages.

Performance Foods

On long treks, nothing perks you up quite as well as a blast from a prepackaged energy snack. The gel types, such as Power-Gel or GU Sports Gel, seem to be just the right size and offer quick energy in an easily ingested form. For a more substantial minimeal, consider the PowerBar, the PowerBar Harvest Bar, Balance Bar, or Cliff Bar.

What I Eat and Carry

As long as it is cooked, boiled, or peeled, I eat whatever the locals eat. Occasionally, however, I crave a little something different. So, for 2- to 3-week treks into remote but inhabited jungle regions, I carry the following supplemental items: one 2-ounce, heavy-duty poly bottle filled with salt and pepper mixed half and half; a few pounds of rice; a tin of long-keeping butter (or a screw-cap plastic bottle of oil) for cooking the rice; a few tins of tuna or sardines packed in tropical hot sauce; and several Power-Gel energy packets for trail snack treats. Much goodwill can be generated by carrying hard caramels to share with porters after long or difficult passages.

Food Safety

In North America and Europe we don't give much thought to the safety of the food we eat; we just assume it is free of risk. Thanks to modern packaging, refrigeration, the use of preservatives, and the standards under which food served in restaurants and at home is prepared, we have little need to worry regarding the transmission of infectious diseases.

In the poorer nations of the world where health and sanitation standards are lax, there is increased risk that food may be contaminated. It may be tainted by human feces in the field because of a lack of latrines for agricultural workers or during the process of food preparation because of inattention to such simple measures as hand washing on the part of food handlers. In many towns and especially in rural areas of the tropics, refrigeration may be nonexistent or unreliable.

It is impossible to ascertain the safety of food through the chain of events from cultivation in the field, transportation to town, preparation, and serving. Here are a few measures to minimize your risk.

Salads Avoid *all* salads. There are special solutions sold throughout third-world countries in which leafy vegetables supposedly can be disinfected by soaking. Don't believe it! As a famous lecturer in tropical medicine always reminded his audience, "The only way to sterilize a salad is with a blowtorch!" Somehow, that has stuck with me.

Vegetables Avoid uncooked vegetables.

Fruits Avoid fruits that you have not yourself peeled.

Dairy Products Avoid unpasteurized milk and milk products such as cheese. Avoid creamy pastries and mayonnaise-based dishes.

Meat and Fish Avoid meat, fish, and shellfish that is undercooked or raw. Having said that, I still eat *ceviche* (raw marinated conch, fish, shrimp, or octopus) at every opportunity. Do as I say, not as I do! Also, cooked items should be *recently* cooked and served hot, not rewarmed.

The rule for minimizing illness from food is simply this: *boil it, peel it, cook it, or forget it!*

POTABLE WATER

As a rule of thumb, all water (other than carbonated, bottled water) in third-world countries should be suspect. Even in large cities and in the best hotels, there is no guarantee that the water is safe to drink. I automatically assume that all nonbottled water that I have not myself treated is unsafe throughout Latin America. Just because the management of your hotel says that the water has been treated and is safe does not mean that, in fact, it is. Also, keep in mind that ice is often made from contaminated water. Freezing contaminated water does not lessen the risk of transmission of certain pathogens. Additionally, remember that hard liquor poured over ice cubes does not kill disease-causing organisms. I don't know how many times I've been sitting at a bar in an international airport and overheard one salesman tell another, "Yeah, I never drink the water in these God-forsaken places. Just booze. Whiskey on the rocks, that's the secret."

I recall the first time the relationship between human waste and contaminated water was made crystal clear to me. I was standing on the bank of the Ucayali River in Pucallpa, Peru, looking at a raft of logs tied off to the riverbank. It was early in the morning and a man started brushing his teeth with water from the river. At the other end of the log raft, less than 25 feet upriver, a young mother appeared with two little boys in tow and an infant in her arms. Both boys had their butts hanging over their end of the raft and were depositing runny, yellow stool into the water. The mother was down on her knees wringing out the baby's cloth diaper into the river. Given the velocity of the current, it was safe to say the man was getting a fairly concentrated dollop of human excrement in his mouth.

Things often aren't much better, really, with regard to the purity of tap water in hotels, restaurants, and homes in some tropical countries. Municipal water systems are often poorly maintained and subject to contamination by human waste. With this background of less than strict standards of sanitation, how can the traveler in third-world countries decrease the risk of consuming contaminated water? Consider the following:

Bottled Water

The process of carbonation kills the pathogens that cause disease in man. Therefore, where available, bottled *carbonated* water is safe. Bottled noncarbonated water is safer than tap water but *not nearly* as safe as carbonated water.

Beer and Wine

These items are safe.

Boiled Water

In the past, it was thought that 5 to 10 minutes of boiling water was necessary to eliminate pathogens. Based on recent field water treatment studies at low altitude, it appears that bringing water to boil and allowing it to boil for an additional minute is sufficient to kill virtually all pathogens.

Iodine

Potable Aqua (tetraglycine hydroperiodide 16.7 percent) tablets are recommended for treating water because they are easy to use and have proved effective in killing bacteria, viruses, and most parasite cysts. Other brand names of iodine also are available.

Books and articles geared for the traveler often advise travelers to obtain clear water, both on aesthetic grounds and from the practical standpoint that cloudy water contaminated with organic material is more difficult to purify. You may read about the desirability of filtration, clarification, sedimentation, and other techniques to remove suspended particles. In the real world, when you are hot, sweaty, and exhausted, it is unlikely you are going to spend a lot of time worrying about such niceties as suspended particulate matter. I try to find water that looks reasonably clear, drop in one Potable Aqua tablet per liter of water, wait 20 to 30 minutes, and drink. If the water looks turbid or just downright nasty, I add a second tablet.

Water Filter

Water filters have gained popularity in recent years and are standard equipment on high-altitude expeditions. Filters are *not* recommended for purifying jungle water; they clog up with silt every few minutes and must be cleaned frequently. If a water filter is used, it should be fitted with a good prefilter to catch the excess silt.

10

HAZARDS (REAL AND IMAGINED)

Arthropods
Fish
Amphibians
Mammals
Reptiles
Plants
Miscellaneous Hazards

Oh stranger from the North, be careful how you tread these jungle paths!

George Dyott, *Manhunting in the Jungle*

The following hazards were chosen for discussion because they are commonly encountered in the wilderness jungle setting—or because people think they are.

ARTHROPODS

Ants

Conga Ant   The conga ant, *Paraponera clavata*, 1 to 1½ inches long, is the terror of the American tropics. The sting from these large, aggressive black ants can produce intense pain and fever for up to 24 hours—hence the Spanish name *veinte-cuatro*—and have been credited with having the most crippling sting of all ants against human beings.

Fortunately, conga ants are conspicuous because their large, shiny black bodies tend to stand out against foliage. Special caution is needed when ducking under or climbing over trees that have fallen over the trail; ants are often found in these fallen trees. For relief of the excruciating pain, a conga bite requires the injection of lidocaine at the bite site and perhaps strong oral pain medication.

Fire Ants Fire ants of the genus *Solenopsis* are common throughout the tropics of South America and have recently spread throughout the southeastern United States. Fire ant stings cause discomfort, but not the unbearable pain of the conga ant. A curious feature of multiple stings from fire ants is the immediate rash that develops, followed within a few hours by vesicles containing clear fluid and, within 24 hours, the formation of sterile pustules. After several days, the pustules rupture or resolve into scabs. There is no good evidence that treatment of run-of-the-mill fire ant stings by antihistamines, steroids, antibiotics, or pustule aspiration alters the natural course of resolution. On the other hand, should the lesions become secondarily infected, oral antibiotic treatment is warranted and, obviously, anaphylactic reactions should be treated with epinephrine (EpiPen Auto Injector).

Army Ants A colony of half a million army ants, genus *Eciton*, on the march is one of the most amazing sights in the world! Despite what Hollywood might have you believe (see the high-camp classic *The Naked Jungle*, starring Charlton Heston), your chances of being devoured by marauding army ants is nil.

When army ants invade huts and homes in the tropics they are more often than not looked upon as *a good thing*. The human inhabitants do not even attempt to turn aside the horde of advancing ants. The people leave, the ants enter the house, and every cockroach, spider, and beetle in the house will be rounded up and eaten. In an hour or so the unstoppable column moves on and the humans return to occupy their homes.

If you happen to be around during an invasion of army ants, step to one side and watch them go at it! If you get too close and a few ants take a bite out of your skin, not to worry—they do not inflict the pain of many other smaller, less ferocious-looking ants.

Other Ants Travelers should avoid touching trees and bushes. Many plants in the tropics harbor colonies of ant "protectors" in a relationship in which the plants provide a home and food for the ants and the ants provide aggressive defense of the plants.

Two classic examples of this remarkable ant-plant mutualism involve plants of the genus *Acacia* and *Cecropia*. In the case of the thorny acacia, the tree provides both shelter and, by means of specialized nutrient-producing structures, food for ants of the genus *Pseudomyrmex*. The ants, in turn, vigorously defend the plant. If you happen to brush up against an acacia, expect to see dozens of stinging ants come pouring out of the hollow thorns! Even the *odor* of nearby humans causes these ants to become active. The cecropia, a tree commonly found where cleared areas have been abandoned, is host to ants of the genus *Azteca*. In return for providing room and board, the cecropia is protected from herbivorous insects and other threatening creatures by the loyal ants, who will enthusiastically and painfully make their presence known.

If you should be attacked by tree-protecting ants, however, put scientific detachment aside, run like hell, slap at the ants that swarm over your body and kill as many of the vicious little beasts as you possibly can. There are billions more where those came from.

Chiggers

Chiggers (trombiculid mite larvae) are a problem throughout the equatorial regions. Whereas temperate-climate chiggers may cause mild discomfort for a few days, the tropical chigger sets up an inflammatory and allergic reaction leading to raging itches that come and go for weeks.

In the South American tropics, chiggers are found in grassy fields such as jungle airstrips and in lawns around mission compounds. Walking through chigger-infested areas without protection could leave a person riddled with chigger bites. After a few days the victim begins to itch mildly. As the days pass, the itching intensifies and comes in waves. For some reason, there seems to be a cycle of virtual cecessation of itching for hours at a time—blessed relief!—then the victim will be overwhelmed by frantic itching at the bite sites. This is especially noticeable and bothersome when these paroxysms of itching hit during the night hours. A curious feature of chigger infestation is that at times the itching seems to be centered in one area, such as the legs, and a few hours later another area, perhaps the armpits, may feel on fire.

Prevention is the best treatment. Areas known to be infested with chiggers should be avoided when possible. Spraying shoes or boots and lower pant legs with repellent containing DEET is somewhat effective. In camp, wearing rubber boots sprayed with DEET greatly reduces the number of bites.

Pretreatment of clothing with permethrin is recommended. Travelers in the American tropics should *never* walk through grassy areas in shorts.

Even if you take the above precautions, in certain regions of South America chiggers will eventually attach themselves to your skin. The closest remedy I have found to ease somewhat the aggravation of chigger bites is Elimite Cream applied to the skin of areas with chigger infestation and left on overnight before washing. I am unaware of any scientific study to support my limited experience using Elimite for this purpose.

Ticks

Few creatures are more successfully adapted to their environment than ticks. They attack all vertebrates except fish and are particularly troublesome to mammals. [T]hey are relatively free from natural enemies, can regenerate lost parts, and have been known to survive without feeding for over 4 years.

C. Schreck, *Wilderness Medicine*, 3rd ed.

Reading the above, you may almost want to wave the white flag of surrender before even entering the field of battle with the wily tick. Aside from the numerous diseases transmitted by ticks, you also have an emotional basis for avoiding them: who wants to deal with a crablike creature bloated to near-bursting with your blood?

Traditional methods for dislodging attached ticks include the application of nail polish, nail polish remover, lighter fluid, oil, or petroleum jelly. Tweezers or commercially available tick removal tools are highly recommended. Place the tips of the tweezers around the area where the mouthparts enter the skin. With a steady, slow motion, pull the tick away from the skin. Do not squeeze or crush the tick. If the mouthparts are left buried in the skin, attempts should be made to remove them to minimize the likelihood of infection or a foreign body reaction. Avoid handling ticks with uncovered fingers.

Jigger Flea

Tunga penetrans, the jigger flea or chigoe, originally was found in South and Central America but now has spread to East and West Africa and India. The fertilized female flea enters the feet through cracks in the soles, between the toes, and around the toenails. The female swells to the size of a pea and may be readily identified as a white papule with a central pit through which the female extrudes excrement and eggs. At about the time the flea eggs are ripe for release, intense itching sets in and the ensuing scratching helps release large numbers of flea eggs.

Inept and incomplete removal of the jigger frequently results in impressive complications due to secondary infection. The following simple extraction technique used by Dr. Ron Guderian, virtually eliminates complications: open the skin over the nest of eggs with a surgical blade. Fold back the flaps, remove the egg sac which is easily identified, and, with tweezers, remove the head of the female flea which can be seen once the egg sac has been removed. Wash the area with hydrogen peroxide.

Local natives are very familiar with the appearance and symptoms of the jigger flea and seldom miss the diagnosis. People living in areas where these fleas are a nuisance have developed expertise in plucking them out without bursting the egg sac. If you lack the confidence to perform the procedure, consider allowing a native to perform the delicate extraction to minimize bursting the egg sac. Although natives usually use a clean palm sliver, you may wish to supply said flea-plucker with a sterile needle.

Myiasis

Myiasis refers to boil-like lesions that occur in the skin of persons infested by larvae of flies. In sub-Saharan Africa, this condition is generally caused by the tumbu fly, *Cordylobia anthropophaga*. The tumbu lays her eggs on clothing or bedding that has been placed on the ground to dry after washing. When clothing containing the fly larvae is worn, the combination of heat and vibration from contact with human skin causes the larvae to penetrate the skin. Clinically, a small, itchy bump, usually on the neck, head, or back, will be noted. This develops over a few days into a boil-like lesion. The breathing organs of the maggot, known as respiratory spiracles, will be seen protruding from the swollen area. Myiasis due to the tumbu fly can be avoided by hanging clothing and bedding to dry in bright sunlight, never on the ground.

In tropical regions of Central and South America, the human botfly, *Dermatobia hominis,* captures a specific species of mosquito in midair, glues her eggs to the underside of the captured insect, then releases the mosquito unharmed. When the mosquito lands on a warm-blooded host—you, for example—the fly larvae emerge from the egg membrane and enter the skin. At first, the victim is unaware of this uninvited guest. By the second week, however, an itchy swelling under the skin develops and a clear or slightly bloody drainage will be noted oozing from the tiny pore through which the developing maggot breathes. Later, as the lesion becomes more . . . well, *juicy* . . . bubbles will be noted coming from the breathing pore and the patient will feel movement under the skin as the larva wriggles around. In the natural course of events, the mature larva emerges from the skin and falls to the ground. Removing the larva before it emerges on its own, however, is generally advised, if only for aesthetic reasons: there is something inherently unpleasant about harboring a moving, growing maggot under the skin.

The diagnostic features of human botfly infection include the following:

1. History of recent travel to Central or South America.

2. One or more dome-shaped boils that contain a pore from which a clear to slightly bloody fluid bubbles.

3. Itching, fleeting sharp pains, and crawling or moving sensations under the skin.

4. On close inspection, a small white structure (the breathing apparatus of the creature) that protrudes from the hole.

Treatment of botfly infestation traditionally involves asphyxiating the larva by covering the breathing pore with pork, chewing gum, petroleum jelly, fingernail polish, or moistened tobacco leaves. One source suggests filling a toothpaste cap with petroleum jelly or fat and securing it over the breathing pore with adhesive tape. Using any of these occlusive means, after a day or two the larvae will be dead or will have wriggled out into the occlusive fat/jelly and can be removed.

Surgical excision should be undertaken with caution because accidental rupture of the larva can lead to secondary infections. The liberal use of insect repellents will help reduce the incidence of human botfly myiasis.

Scorpions and Spiders

Stinging scorpions and venomous spiders are common throughout the tropics and provide yet another reason to exercise caution before sitting down or placing a hand on logs, bushes, or the ground.

If anything in nature fairly shrieks *"Leave me alone!"* it is definitely the scorpion. With its lobsterlike front claws and prominent tail terminating in a conspicuous stinger, these arthropods exhibit an unusually vigilant aspect as they track your every movement. Fortunately for the jungle traveler, notoriously deadly scorpions tend to inhabit desert and semiarid regions of the Middle East and northern Africa. Potentially lethal scorpions (genus *Tityus*), however, also occur throughout South America, particularly in Brazil.

Scorpions are nocturnal feeders and like to hide in ground debris, under old wood and, unfortunately, in shoes and sleeping gear. Prevention of painful scorpion stings should include checking shoes and clothing left outside and avoiding campsites where there is a lot of dead wood and desiccated leaves.

There are over 30,000 species of spiders scattered throughout the world. Almost all spiders have venom glands, but only a few dozen possess fangs sufficient to penetrate human skin or venom of sufficient potency to produce significant symptoms in humans.

The South American banana spider (genus *Phoneutria*), also known as the wandering spider or "aranha armadeira" (spider that assumes an armed display), is notorious for its aggressive behavior and exquisitely painful bite! This gray to brown-gray spider is huge, with a leg span of up to 12 cm and fangs that are 5 mm in length.

This spider's venom is complex and includes histamine, serotonin, glutamic acid, aspartic acid, lysine, and hydraluronidase. The neurotoxic components are sodium channel poisons that provoke erratic and rapid, uncontrolled muscle twitches. After envenomation the patient experiences truly intense local pain at the bite site and may develop rapid heart rate, profuse sweating, salivation, dizziness, visual disturbances, nausea, vomiting, and, in the case of preadolescent boys, an erection! Death is a rare occurrence.

On the night of January 30, 1999, while camped in the region of the headwaters of the Padamo River in Amazonas State, Venezuela, I made two mistakes that led to my being bitten by a banana spider. Against my initial instincts, I slung my hammock over the dried leaves and debris-strewn ground beneath an abandoned shelter Yanomami and Cobaliwa Indians had used on past hunting and fishing expeditions. Early in the night I placed my rubber camp boots on the ground beside the hammock and was about to fade into a deep sleep when the urge to urinate struck. Half-asleep, I sat up on the edge of the hammock, picked up a boot *which had fallen over on its side onto the ground*, and plunged my foot into the boot without so much as a shake or inspection. Big mistake! In the first millisecond of a sudden jabbing pain on my second toe I thought a scorpion had struck. Then, a moment later when the second pain seized my little toe and I felt movement in the boot I considered a small snake. I jerked my foot out of the boot, turned the boot upside down, and out staggered an enormous, slightly stunned spider that plopped onto the ground. (Note: any spider that has enough mass to make a sound when it hits the ground is bad news.) Not recognizing this spider at the time and lacking anything better to do as I waited to see what would happen next, I kept notes, as best as I could under the circumstances.

- 9:50 P.M. Bites to the second and small toe of my right foot. The most severe pain I have ever experienced, including the passage of two kidney stones.

- 10:00 P.M. Second toe and little toe are significantly swollen and my whole foot is numb.

- 1:30 A.M. The pain in my right foot remains incredibly agonizing. My whole foot has a tingling sensation. I have a curious, seemingly contradictory set of sensations of my foot: numbness and pain simultaneously on the dorsum of the foot and a slightly moist sensation, although the moistness is not confirmed by actual touch. No redness or heat. Pulse 56 beats per minute (my normal pulse is 56–64). I have a recurrent, severe muscle cramp of my left (not right) calf.

- 4:00 A.M. The swelling of my foot nearly gone. I continue to have swelling of the two toes.

Over a period of several hours during the night I experienced odd paresthesias of the left side of my face; that is, a distinct sense that something like hair, or a spiderweb or the sensation of someone lightly moving their fingertips over my skin. I repeatedly rubbed my face with my hand or rubbed my face against the hammock in an effort to "brush away" the phantom sensation.

As in the case of scorpion stings, prevention of painful spider bites should include avoidance of campsites where there is a lot of dead wood and desiccated leaves; shoes should be checked for spiders before being placed on the feet.

Treat banana spider bites with local infiltration of lidocaine. Do not use opioid narcotics; these drugs can worsen the venom's effect of depressing respiration. In Brazil, a polyvalent antivenom is available. The effectiveness of this injectable antivenom is judged by relief of pain and the subsidence of erection!

Venomous Moths, Butterflies, and Caterpillars

The larvae and adults of a number of moths (genus *Hylesia*) and butterflies bear venomous hairs that may cause skin eruptions. The rash may result from direct contact with the adults or larvae or by windblown hairs. The pain resulting from direct contact with certain Amazonian caterpillars can be excruciating and disabling.

In the Amazon tropics, noxious smoke from the burning of garbage (such as the plastic wrappers of freeze-dried food) may cause tree-dwelling caterpillars to loosen their hold on overhead branches and rain down on unwary campers below.

Treatment of lepidoptera envenomation may require injection of lidocaine at the site of intense pain and the administration of analgesics, antihistamines, and corticosteroids. Moth hairs may be removed with the sticky rolling lint removers used for clothing.

Wasp and Bee Stings

The sudden, intense pain from the sting of certain species of tropical wasps and bees can be so severe that it knocks the victim to the ground as though hit with an electric shock. Wearing of perfumes and brightly colored or flower-patterned clothing should be avoided. I am convinced that some individuals, regardless of what they wear, are more likely to get stung than others. Birdwatchers should not venture too close to the hanging nests of yellow-rumped caciques and oropendolas because wasps are invariably associated with these nests.

FISH

Stingray

The stingray, a flattened, cartilaginous cousin of the shark, may be encountered buried just beneath the surface of the bottom ooze in tropical rivers and streams throughout the Amazon Basin, Africa, and Indochina. Rays inflict injury by lashing upward with the tail, driving a retro-serrated venomous spine deep into the victim's foot, ankle, or lower leg. This produces agonizing pain often accompanied by headache, vomiting, and shortness of breath. After the initial phase of envenomation passes, tissue death may set in. Indians inhabiting the Amazon Basin, who fear little, truly dread the thought of an encounter with a stingray.

Wearing shoes or boots when wading in water does not always prevent the stingray from jabbing its barb into the foot or leg. Prevention lies in shuffling the feet along the bottom so that the ray will have enough warning to glide away safely.

First aid consists of using copious amounts of salt water or clean fresh water to irrigate the wound in order to flush out and dilute the venom. When the pain is intense, local infiltration of the wound with 1 percent lidocaine (without epinephrine) is useful.

The late Dr. H. Alistair Reid, a longtime lecturer at the Liverpool School of Tropical Medicine, gave the following suggestions for managing the pain associated with a variety of envenomations:

"The most effective treatment for the local pain of venomous stings . . . is hot water. The part stung is immersed in water as hot as the patient can bear (and only the patient can decide how

hot this is). The pain is relieved within seconds and the part stung must be quickly removed from the water to avoid blistering. It should be reimmersed as pain recurs (within seconds at first, later within minutes). This procedure should be continued until the pain no longer recurs (usually about half an hour)." (Reid, Management and Treatment of Tropical Diseases.)

Patients should have a tetanus booster if they have not had one in the past 10 years. Administration of an antibiotic such as trimethoprim-sulfamethoxazole or ciprofloxin twice daily for one week is advised.

Electric Eel

The so-called electric eel (actually an eel-shaped fish) is encountered from Guatemala to the La Plata River in South America and is especially common in the Amazon region. A person can drown after being stunned by the jolt this fish delivers.

Electric eels are said to prefer deep water. Inhabitants of regions heavily infested with these fish report that a slight tingling sensation of the skin may be felt when one is close at hand. No practical way of preventing these shocks is known, although legends tell of explorers in years past driving horses through infested waters so the eels discharged their "batteries" and were rendered harmless to humans wading in the river. Whether true or not, it makes a rather good story.

Candiru

The candiru is a toothpick-sized parasitic catfish that inhabits Amazonian waters and may invade the urethra of humans who are urinating. Orifice penetration by the candiru can be prevented by wearing a tight bathing suit and not urinating underwater. The author Redmond O'Hanlon feared this fish so much that he invented an anti-candiru device using a tea strainer to fit over his penis! (Somehow, this seems entirely fitting for someone from the United Kingdom.) There are various native methods of dislodging these fish from the urethra, including drinking a tea made from the green fruit of the *jugua* tree, *Genipa americana L*. Two to five grams of vitamin C taken by mouth may serve the same purpose.

Piranha

As previously noted, there are no confirmed human deaths resulting from piranha attack. These fish have, however, nipped off the fingertips of canoeists who carelessly dangled their hands in the water in a sort of trolling mode.

AMPHIBIANS

Poison-dart Frogs

Poison-dart frogs—tiny, brilliantly colored species in the genus *Dendrobates*—may be encountered in Central America and northern South America. *Phyllobates terribilis,* restricted to the vicinity of the Rio Patia in southwestern Colombia, secretes a toxin from its skin that is so powerful, a lethal dose could be absorbed if enough of the skin secretion of the frog came into contact with an open wound. It is wise to avoid all contact with brilliantly colored frogs, caterpillars, and snakes.

MAMMALS

Bats

Vampire bats are found throughout Mexico, Central America, and South America, especially in areas that have large cattle ranches. Sleeping humans are unaware of the presence of a feeding bat; the phlebotomy is painless. Both vampire and fruit bats carry rabies. Sleeping under mosquito netting prevents bat bites. The risk of rabies can be reduced by prophylactic human diploid cell vaccine.

Dogs

Most native groups keep dogs around for hunting. Populations with a history of recent tribal warfare often keep packs of dogs close by as an early warning system. These semiwild dogs should be treated with caution; threatening them may cause immediate attack, since they are not easily intimidated. When approaching huts or villages, the traveler should allow porters to go first so they can deal with the dogs.

Dogs that are intent on biting often adopt particular behavior patterns. The traveler should be hyper-vigilant of the dog that, when protecting its territory, crouches low, straightens its back and tail, emits a deep guttural growl, and stares fixedly at a specific part of the person's anatomy. When such behavior is observed, an attack is imminent. At this point a sharp blow to the dog's nose with your foot or a stick may be the only way to deflect the attack. Some dog experts recommend freezing in place as a way of avoiding attack by a dog whose space has been invaded. It is best to avoid making direct eye contact with a dog that exhibits aggressive behavior.

Jaguars

Jaguar attacks on humans are exceedingly rare. The following recommendations for deterring a jaguar attack are based on advice for avoiding a cougar attack: increase your apparent size by raising your arms above your head and waving an object such as a backpack or stick or opening a jacket; yell, shout, or speak loudly and forcefully in a low, deep tone of voice; back away slowly; do *not* turn your back and run.

REPTILES

Snakes

Snakebites are rare; 450,000 person-hours of field work at sites in Costa Rican rainforests were documented without a single snakebite.

Most poisonous snakes tend to blend into their surroundings, and nonnatives rarely see them. This fact is the basis for the most effective protection: *put a jungle-reared guide in front on the trail.* Natives almost always spot a poisonous snake and can quickly dispatch it.

Snakes are often encountered along the shoreline of rivers and small streams. Particular caution is needed when hiking in such areas or when disembarking from a canoe or rubber raft. In the forest the hiker should always step up onto a log and then step away from the log: it should not be straddled (snakes often are encountered where the log makes contact with the jungle floor). Since many venomous snakes in the tropics are heat-seeking and hunt at night, caution is needed when walking around in camp at night. Trips to the toilet after dark should be kept to a minimum.

Anacondas (water boas) feature in the folklore of all native cultures in the regions of Amazonia where these enormous snakes (up to 30 feet long) live. These nonpoisonous snakes kill by looping coils around prey and then tightening the coils, suffocating the victim. There are anecdotal reports of anacondas attacking and swallowing humans, particularly children and women bathing at the edge of a jungle stream, but such stories are unconfirmed.

Major Snake Families The venomous snakes of tropical regions of the Americas, sub-Saharan Africa, and Southeast Asia can be divided into the following major snake families: *Atractaspididae*—the burrowing asps of Africa; *Elapidae*—the coral snakes, mambas, and cobras found in various regions of the tropical world; *Hydrophiidae*—the sea snakes of Southeast Asia and the coastal waters of Australia; and *Viperidae*—the pit vipers of the Americas and Asia and the Old World vipers of Africa and Asia. The text *Wilderness Medicine* has excellent discussions of the most important species of venomous snakes in various regions of the world.

In the Americas, the pit vipers, particularly the "fer-de-lance" (several species of the genus *Bothrops*), the dreaded "bushmaster"

(*Lachesis muta*), and species of mostly green, tree-dwelling snakes, pose the greatest threat. Bites from coral snakes (Elapids in the genus *Micrurus*) are exceedingly rare.

Recognition of Envenomation For a number of reasons, pit vipers may release full amounts of venom or little or no venom ("dry bite") in any given bite. Occasionally, when snakes strike, clothing or shoes deflect the strike and no envenomation occurs. Remember, fang marks (which may appear as well-defined punctures or as small lacerations or scratches) are observed in nearly 100 percent of instances where there has been envenomation, but the presence of fang marks does not necessarily imply that envenomation occurred. For snakebite victims who may be hours or days from definitive medical treatment, it is of interest to know if, in fact, there was actual envenomation. *Pit viper envenomation* in the Americas can be assumed by the following:

1. Swelling and burning pain at the site of the bite. The swelling usually begins within minutes after the bite, although on occasion these local findings may not be evident right away.

2. Weakness.

3. Nausea and vomiting.

4. Tingling or prickling sensations (paresthesias) of the face, lips, and extremities.

5. Bleeding at the bite site and occasionally from the mouth and nose. Also, blisters may form at the bite site.

Severe pit viper envenomation—for example, where venom has been injected into a blood vessel—may be recognized by the rapid development of low blood pressure and shock.

Coral snakes have small mouths, very short fangs, and envenomate in a sort of chewing manner. These shy creatures rarely bite unless provoked. Coral snakes and their nonpoisonous mimics have beautifully colored bands, usually red, black, and yellow. The rule of "red on yellow, kill a fellow; red on black, venom lack" is true only for the coral snakes of the southern United States and northern Mexico. Venomous coral snake species encountered south of Mexico City and throughout Central America and South America cannot be excluded by the "red on black, venom lack" rule.

Coral snake venom is predominantly neurotoxic and envenomation by coral snakes may be suspected by these findings:

1. The bitten limb usually will feel weak or numb within an hour to an hour and a half.

2. Tingling sensations and twitching of muscles of the bitten limb.

3. Increased salivation and drooling within hours.

4. Slurred speech and double vision within 5 to 10 hours.

Envenomation by pit vipers is virtually always accompanied by the rapid onset of local pain and swelling and visible fang marks. In the case of coral snakes, fang marks may be difficult to identify. Evidence of envenomation may not be apparent for hours and may or may not be accompanied by local pain and swelling. Severe envenomation is characterized by impaired breathing, paralysis, and death from heart and lung failure.

I recall discussing snakes and envenomation with my Shuar Indian friend and guide, Daniel Cashindo, as we trekked along the Rio Huasaga in eastern Ecuador. After reviewing the common pit vipers and local remedies for snakebite, I said, "Tell me about coral snakebites." "They almost never bite anyone," he replied. "Well, if they *do* bite, what do you do?" He continued down the trail and without skipping a beat said, "You die."

Medical Management of Snakebite When Prompt Evacuation to a Trauma Center Is Possible In situations—admittedly rare in developing nations—where it is possible to promptly transport the victim to a major trauma center properly equipped to deal with snake envenomation, there are a few first aid measures that should be executed without delay.

Dr. Terence Davidson, professor of surgery at the University of California San Diego, has developed protocols so that emergency room or trauma physicians can manage snakebite appropriately. Physicians who plan to serve as an "expedition doctor" would be well advised to review Dr. Davidson's discussion (*www-surgery.ucsd.edu/ENT/DAVIDSON/snake*) of the management of envenomation for the snakes likely to be encountered in any region of the world.

The following immediate first aid recommendations are adapted from Dr. Terry Davidson's web page:

1. Make sure the snake has been safely contained and can no longer inflict any additional bites.

2. Immediately call for transportation.

3. Keep the victim calm and reassured. Allow him or her to lie flat and avoid as much movement as possible. If possible, allow the bitten limb to rest at a level lower than the victim's heart.

4. Identify the bite site, looking for fang marks, and apply the Sawyer pump Extractor with the largest cup possible over the bite site.

5. Immediately wrap a constricting band snugly about the bitten limb at a level just above the bite site, that is, between the bite site and the heart. The constricting band should be as tight as one might bind a sprained ankle, but not so tight as to constrict blood flow. For constriction, Dr. Davidson recommends a 1-inch penrose drain of the type commonly used for venipuncture. (As another option, an ACE bandage wrapped snugly—but not too tightly—around the bitten limb will provide excellent constriction while the victim is being transported to a hospital. Even better, apply one ACE around the bitten extremity, then cradle the limb in a SAM splint and apply a second ACE around the SAM splint to hold it in place. A stick or folded newspaper, though not as elegant as a SAM splint, will serve the purpose in a pinch.)

6. *Do not* remove the constricting band until the victim has reached the hospital and is receiving antivenin.

7. *Do not* cut or incise the bite site.

8. *Do not* apply ice to the bite site.

How to Handle a Snakebite When You Can't Get to a Trauma Center It is tempting to give some sort of definitive recommendation for management of snakebite for situations where the victim cannot be immediately transported to a major health center for appropriate care. Unfortunately, as of this writing, there is *no* consensus on proven, effective management of snakebite under such circumstances. In fact, several experts categorically recommend that visitors to isolated jungle regions *not* carry antivenin. (It is not well known by most travelers or, for that matter, by many physicians, that treatment of pit viper envenomation usually requires 15 to 20 vials of antivenin at a cost of over $500 per vial! In addition, there are potentially serious immediate and delayed systemic reactions possible when using currently available antivenin.)

Until a cheaper, more stable antivenin is available, the following suggestions should be considered regarding snake envenomation in truly remote areas of wilderness in third-world countries:

1. *Avoid being bitten.* Always travel with a native guide leading the way on the trail to spot and thus avoid venomous snakes.

2. *Extractor pump.* Use the Sawyer Extractor within seconds or minutes of being bitten. Note: there is little if any scientific evidence the extractor actually works! On the other hand, it probably does no harm and may provide some psychologic boost to the victim and to the caregiver who feels the need to *do something*.

3. *Evacuation.* Many experts agree that, once envenomated, the best plan is to carry good communications gear to call for help and hope to hell you can get out quickly by helicopter, plane, or high-speed boat!

Alligators and Crocodiles

The Guayas and its tributaries are full of alligators. The natives do not seem to be troubled by their proximity, though it is admitted they do chew incautious children.

Edward Whymper, *Travels Amongst the Great Andes of the Equator*

Alligators and crocodiles appear torpid as they lie sunning themselves. Such creatures can move amazingly fast when they want to; crocodiles reportedly can travel in the water at a speed of 20 mph and charge over land at up to 30 mph. Humans cannot outswim or outrun a charging crocodile.

Bites should be treated with thorough cleaning of the wound, surgical debridement if necessary, tetanus prophylaxis, and an appropriate antibiotic. A study of the oral flora of 10 alligators captured in Louisiana revealed various aerobic and anaerobic organisms responsive to trimethoprim-sulfamethoxazole.

PLANTS

Armed or Spine-Bearing Plants

Spine-bearing plants abound in forested areas of the tropics. The peach palm, *Bactris gasipaes,* a tall, slender palm whose palmheart and fruit mesocarp are much prized by natives, is found from Nicaragua to Bolivia. The trunk of the tree is ringed with needle-sharp spines. Peach palms often grow alongside trails. Contact with this palm can drive spines deep into the flesh. Spines that enter a joint space may require surgical extraction. Secondary infection and an inflammatory response often occur.

Hallucinogenic Plants

There are very real psychological risks incurred from ingesting the powerful intoxicating agents used by tribal populations inhabiting the tropical lowlands of Central and South America. The effects of some of these drugs—ayahuasca, for example—can be quite unsettling and the memory of the experience long lasting. An American physician who ingested ayahuasca on only one occasion recalls, decades later, vivid hallucinations in which the houses bordering the street of the jungle town where he took the drug all turned a chalky blue, seemed to come to life, and began to expand and contract as though breathing, so that he had the distinct impression he would be crushed if he did not get off the street immediately.

My advice is to avoid these drugs.

Sawgrass

In many regions of the tropics, sawgrass is an ever-present nuisance. Blades of this grass can slice into exposed skin like a surgical scalpel. Even when treated with antibiotic ointment, the lacerations often take 1 to 2 weeks to heal. Hikers should carefully avoid touching sawgrass; special care is needed when working with a machete.

Falling Trees

Tropical trees do not have deep roots and often fall in relatively modest winds. In many regions of the world the risk of snakebite is probably lower than the risk of injury or death from falling trees.

Little can be done to anticipate or avoid trees that fall in a windstorm or simply because they are old and rotted. In the forest, hammocks should be slung away from large trees. Travelers setting up camp should always look up at the branches of trees near camp; although the base of the tree may appear sound, areas high up may be rotted.

MISCELLANEOUS HAZARDS

Fording Rivers

The hiker should never attempt to cross a fast-flowing or deep river with a pack on the back. If you do cross with a pack, at least unclip your waist-belt to ensure a speedy release from the pack if you fall. Regaining footing in a rapidly moving current can be difficult. Unless experienced in crossing such streams, the traveler should take the hand of a native guide or porter.

Log Bridges

As previously noted in Chapter 1, log bridges present a distinct hazard to trekkers who are unaccustomed to traversing a long, narrow log some 10 to 20 feet above a creek or ravine. Covel Ice Walker Quick Clip Cleats help tremendously in maintaining sure-footedness. A backpack seems to significantly impair balance on logs. If you do not have a porter to carry your backpack and other gear, scoot across on your buttocks.

If holds are at hand, they are usually made of woven lianas and, unless newly installed, prone to rot and break with no warning. Do not put weight on ropelike handholds when crossing log bridges. Instead, lightly touch the handholds only to maintain balance. If you find yourself tipping off the log, it is better to instantly straddle the log than seek support in the weak handholds.

Mercury Contamination

Travelers to certain tropical regions, particularly the Amazon Basin, should be aware of the serious, widespread contamination of waterways by mercury that gold miners use to process their ore. Although most manufacturers of commonly available portable water treatment and filtration systems do not specifically claim to remove mercury, any activated carbon system should reduce the risk. The makers of SafeWater Anywhere (*www.safewateranywhere.com*), a 1-liter squeeze bottle filter, advertise test results showing 99.25 percent mercury removal. Travelers should exercise caution in choosing rivulets as a source of potable water in areas where mercury contamination is known or suspected.

Rising Rivers

Streams, particularly narrow ones bounded by vertical banks, can rise 15 or more feet in a few hours as a result of intense rains. Camps should not be set up on an island or beach in a small canyon during the rainy season. A cloudburst in the headwaters can send a wall of water rushing downstream even though it may be a clear, moonlit night at the campsite.

Revolutions, Minor Uprisings, and Strikes

What to do if you happen to be in a city during a time of serious unrest? I suggest you check into the best, most expensive hotel in town and stay put until the smoke clears. There are several reasons to choose the best hotel: First, since the electricity in the city will almost certainly be cut off, you will not be left in the dark; deluxe hotels have their own power generators. It's nice to have light and even a cold drink when all hell breaks loose on the streets. Furthermore, you can be sure members of the international press corps will be holed up in a first-class establishment. Most would-be coup leaders tend to avoid hurting members of the press.

If fighting is uncomfortably close, it is best to avoid standing in windows or climbing to the roof of the hotel to have a look at the action. Lone figures on the top of buildings are at risk of being picked off by snipers on both sides of the argument.

With all due respect to student readers of this book: get as far away as you can from anyone who looks like a local student. Students are often instigators in nonmilitary takeovers or targets in military takeovers.

Anyone who has spent much time in third-world nations has probably been subjected to minor uprisings and paralyzing strikes. At the least these matters involve inconvenience, and, occasionally, they have the potential of bodily harm from mob violence. If caught in such a situation, get the advice of "old hands," nationals or expatriates, on how to proceed. They have probably been through this countless times and have a feel for how things are going. They can advise you where to hole up or suggest ways of getting to your destination with minimal risk if you feel the need to move around.

Tear Gas Tear gas agents, also known as lacrimators, short-term incapacitants, or harassing agents, are designed to produce immediate disabling effects.

There are three agents commonly in use today: chloroacetophenone, commonly known as CN or Tear Gas Mace; chlorobenzylidene malononitrile, known as CS; and dibenzoxapine, known as CR. All three agents cause varying degrees of immediate eye pain, tearing, stinging of the skin, salivation, and trouble breathing. Some agents cause nausea and vomiting.

Treatment of tear gassing consists of decontamination. The eyes should be washed out using clean water for 5 to 10 minutes and exposed areas of skin should be thoroughly washed with soap and water. Any skin rash that results from Mace contact may require treatment with topical steroids such as hydrocortisone. Clothing should be removed and washed.

More often than not you can prevent accidental exposure to tear gas by following common-sense precautions:

1. If there is known social and political unrest, stay indoors— especially on May Day in Latin American countries. May Day is frequently marked by labor protests that turn violent and authorities often resort to tear gas for crowd control.

2. Avoid universities and the neighborhood around the U.S. Embassy during labor and student unrest. Usually the local newspapers have given ample warning of impending trouble.

3. Take a taxi. Older, more mature taxi drivers are used to clashes between the police/military and students/strikers in countries with a history of political instability and generally know how to avoid troubled areas. Young taxi drivers may go out of their way to pass close by a riot zone!

4. Recognize the peculiar "pop" tear gas launchers make. Go the other way.

5. Many types of tear gas are accompanied by visible white smoke. Head in the opposite direction if you spot smoke coming from an area where there are crowds and an unusually large number of military or police vehicles.

MEDICAL CONCERNS IN THE TROPICS

HEALTH RISKS TO TRAVELERS
Overview
Diseases of Poverty
Travelers' Diarrhea
Epidemiology
   Clinical Manifestations
   Prevention
   Treatment
Malaria
Epidemiology
   Clinical Manifestations
   Diagnosis
   Prevention
   Treatment

WOMEN IN THE JUNGLE
Health Issues
Pregnancy

TRAVELING WITH CHILDREN IN THE TROPICS
Guidelines for Traveling with Children

11

HEALTH RISKS TO TRAVELERS

OVERVIEW

When many people think of tropical regions, they think about tropical diseases and conjure up dramatic images of South Sea Islanders suffering from elephantiasis with legs swollen to the size of a man's trunk. Or they recall from a college parasitology course the classic photo of the fellow whose scrotum was so big he had to carry it around in a wheelbarrow. Although travelers in the tropical forests may have potential *exposure* to numerous serious exotic diseases, the risk of actually coming down with something truly dreadful is very low.

I once made an extensive review of the medical literature on health risks for travelers to third-world countries. It soon became apparent that most of the risk tables were compiled from data obtained from travelers to urban areas and the relatively healthy regions frequented by tourists. Refocusing my search to data on health risks among groups working in fairly isolated regions—U.S. Peace Corps volunteers, anthropologists, and missionaries—it became clear that the major health risks were *motor vehicle accidents* getting to and from jungle regions (particularly if you use a motorcycle as your primary mode of transportation), *hepatitis,* and *malaria.* Looking just at Peace Corps data, it is instructive to note that the risk of dying while serving in the Peace Corps is only 1 per 1,000: unintentional injury (motor vehicle accidents) accounted for 70 percent of deaths; illness made up 21 percent; homicide 4 percent; and, interestingly, suicide 5 percent.

Reviewing the literature and factoring in my own experiences over 35 years in remote regions of the tropics, I have come to the following conclusions regarding relative risk in the tropics:

- *Exposure* to life-threatening disease: moderate risk

- *Death* (from any cause): extremely low risk

- *Diarrhea* or other annoyance: extremely high risk

DISEASES OF POVERTY

To maintain perspective, it helps to keep in mind that when we talk about killer diseases (that is, diseases that are the major killers among native residents) in the tropics we are talking about *diseases of poverty,* rarely exotic tropical diseases.

GEOGRAPHIC DIFFERENCES IN "KILLER" DISEASE PREVALENCE

United States	Africa, Asia, Latin America
1. Heart Disease	1. Diarrheal diseases
2. Malignant neoplasms	2. Respiratory infections
3. Cerebrovascular diseases	3. Malaria
4. Accidents	4. Measles
5. Chronic obstructive pulmonary disease	5. *Schistosomiasis*
6. Suicides, homicides	6. Whooping cough
7. Pneumonia and influenza	7. Tuberculosis
8. Diabetes	8. Neonatal tetanus
9. Chronic liver disease	9. Diphtheria
10. Infant mortality	10. Hookworm

Take a moment to review the above chart. In the left-hand column of the geographic differences in disease prevalence (compiled in the 1980s), you will see the top 10 "killers" in the United States, and in the right-hand column, the top 10 in Africa, Asia, and Latin America. Review the list carefully. Nowhere, other than in the case of schistosomiasis, do you encounter a single exotic parasitic disease that occurs only in the tropics. The common causes of death in the third world today are essentially diseases that were extremely prevalent in the United States (excluding schistosomiasis) in the early 1900s. Keep in mind that malaria is not exclusive to the tropics. Prior to successful eradication campaigns in the rich nations, malaria was common in temperate climates, and in the United States was encountered as far north as the U.S.–Canadian border.

As my mentor and friend, Dr. Ernie Chick, used to remind medical students, the greatest decline of death rates in the United States has resulted from the application of appropriate principles of sanitation and preventive medicine. Diseases in underdeveloped countries reflect the lack of proper sanitation, of supplies of pure food and water, of appropriate immunizations, and control of disease-carrying insects. Overcrowding and inappropriate health practices also contribute to the burden of disease in third-world countries. The difference in the levels of sanitation and the availability and quality of health care between the rich and poor nations is based in large part on money to finance these functions and the development and maintenance of an infrastructure for health care delivery. In many third-world nations, ministries of health have only $10 per person per year to spend on health care needs; in some desperately poor nations, as little as 50 cents is allocated per person per year for health care. Viewed in this fashion, it is easy to grasp the uphill battle faced by poor nations in funding essential health and sanitation needs.

Even in rich nations, a momentary glitch in maintenance of water supplies can have disastrous consequences: in 1993 a massive outbreak of watery diarrhea affecting more than 400,000 people occurred in Milwaukee when cryptosporidium oocysts passed through the filtration system of one of the city's water-treatment plants. Imagine how easy it would be for contamination of water supplies to occur in towns in the tropics where maintenance of equipment is a low priority and where utility employees may have little incentive to even show up for work.

TRAVELERS' DIARRHEA

During my first few years of jaunts into the tropics, I think I had virtually every form of diarrheal illness known to man. I had common travelers' diarrhea due to *E. coli* so many times I eventually developed a semi-immune status; I became *very* familiar with the gaseous, odorific symptoms associated with *Giardia lamblia;* I suffered from the occasional bout of staph food poisoning (mostly a vomiting illness, but occasionally with some diarrhea) from consuming third-world cream-filled pastries, and I got so used to attacks of watery diarrhea from *Vibrio parahaemolyticus,* I swear I think I can smell contaminated shellfish a mile away.

The following will help you understand and minimize illness due to diarrhea-producing organisms.

Epidemiology

Travelers' diarrhea, characterized by a twofold or greater increase in the frequency of unformed bowel movements, is by far the most common illness befalling the traveler.

Attack rates of 20 to 50 percent have been reported in the medical literature for travelers visiting high-risk destinations including Central and South America, Africa, Southeast Asia, and the Indian subcontinent. My experience for off-the-beaten-path travel indicates that attack rates seem to be dependent on 1) the amount of time spent in the frontier towns one passes through to get to true wilderness (the longer you linger in such places, the more likely you are to get diarrhea); 2) the care one exercises in avoiding contaminated food and water; and 3) luck.

Travelers' diarrhea is caused by a variety of bacteria, viruses, and parasites and is encountered worldwide where standards of sanitation are not enforced. These organisms gain access into our intestinal tracts through food or water that has been contaminated by human feces. Any food, whether cooked or uncooked, if improperly handled can be implicated. Raw or undercooked meat, seafood, raw fruits and vegetables, tap water, ice, and unpasteurized milk and dairy products are especially chancy. Where the food is prepared is an important variable: the highest risk is from food sold by street vendors and the lowest risk is from private homes; food sold in restaurants poses an intermediate risk.

Percentagewise, most travelers who develop diarrhea experience only a few days of loose, watery stool; approximately 15 percent will develop a more serious infection with fever and bloody stools (dysentery); only 2 percent develop a chronic diarrhea lasting longer than 1 month.

Clinical Manifestations

Travelers' diarrhea (often dubbed *turista,* Montezuema's revenge, or Aztec quick step by travelers south of the U.S. border), has its onset within a few days after arrival in a foreign country. The patient experiences several days of loose, watery stools, accompanied by nausea, abdominal cramping, bloating and, occasionally, vomiting, and a low-grade fever. Generally, this is a nonbloody form of diarrheal illness, although infection with some organisms may cause bloody diarrhea.

Bacteria The bacterial pathogen known as Enterotoxigenic *Escherichia coli* (ETEC), is the most common causative agents of travelers' diarrhea. Typically, ETEC produces a watery, nonbloody diarrhea that is associated with cramps (at times rather severe) with little or no fever. Untreated, ETEC diarrhea is self-limited, usually lasting 2 to 3 days.

Salmonella gastroenteritis (caused by numerous salmonella serotypes), is characterized by fever, abdominal cramps, and diarrhea, which is sometimes bloody. *Shigella* species cause a watery diarrhea or diarrhea stool mixed with blood and mucus, crampy abdominal pain, and fever. These patients often strain to defecate and appear "toxic." *Campylobacter* is a common cause of diarrhea (often bloody) throughout the world. *Vibrio parahaemolyticus* causes an acute watery diarrhea accompanied by crampy abdominal pain and fever; this condition is caused by ingestion of raw or poorly cooked shellfish, particularly oysters. There are numerous, less common, bacterial pathogens associated with travelers' diarrhea.

Viruses Viruses, particularly rotavirus and Norwalk-like viruses, have been implicated as causes of travelers' diarrhea in adults. *Note:* the live virus vaccine for rotavirus, Rotashield, is no longer available in the United States due to the strong association between the vaccine and bowel obstruction (intussusception) in infants.

Parasites Parasitic pathogens that cause diarrhea in travelers include *Giardia lamblia*, *Entamoeba histolytica*, *Cryptosporidium*, and the recently described parasites, *Cyclospora cayetanensis.*

Giardiasis, caused by the protozoan *Giardia lamblia*, is one of the most common intestinal parasitic diseases encounted in the tropics. Infections are generally transmitted by the waterborne route and occasionally by person-to-person contact or in food. Infection may be asymptomatic or patients may complain of bloating, cramping abdominal pains, and diarrheal stool which is incredibly foul-smelling, yellow, frothy, and floats. Giardiasis is treated using metronidazole (Flagyl) 250 mg three times daily for 5 days. Outside the United States, other drugs such as ornidazole and tinidazole are available for the treatment of giardiasis.

Prevention

Because travelers' diarrhea is contracted through the ingestion of water or food that has been contaminated by feces, it helps to follow the general preventive recommendations noted throughout this book: drink only bottled, carbonated water or water that has been boiled or chemically treated, and consume food that has been cooked or boiled or in the case of fruit, that you have peeled yourself. Despite your best efforts, however, a sojourn into the tropics may be temporarily disrupted by a bout of diarrhea.

Pepto-Bismol, two tablets 4 times a day for up to 3 weeks, has been shown to decrease the incidence of diarrhea by approximately 60 percent in several controlled studies. Actually, it has been my experience that 1 tablet 4 times daily seems to work about as well. Ideally, Pepto-Bismol should be taken with food to be effective. Beware that Pepto-Bismol may turn the tongue and stool black and cause ringing in the ears. It is generally agreed by specialists who run travelers' clinics that the risks of taking antibiotics for prophylaxis outweigh the benefits for a self-limited illness which, though annoying, is not life-threatening. Additionally, prophylatic antibiotics may induce a false sense of security in travelers, making them more likely to commit a food and beverage indiscretion after arrival in a third-world country.

Treatment

There are a number of approaches to the treatment of simple travelers' diarrhea. Here are mine.

At the first sign of gut grumbling, I immediately start with Pepto-Bismol, two tablets 4 times daily for 2 to 3 days. Usually, after the first couple of doses I begin to sense that the Pepto-Bismol is gaining the upper hand. Also, I eat two bowls of rice each day for as long as I have loose stool. If, however, I don't seem to be making satisfactory progress, I begin taking Cipro (ciprofloxacin) 500 mg tablets twice daily for 3 days. Ofloxacin in a dose of 300 mg twice daily for 3 days can be substituted for Cipro as can levofloxacin (Levaquin) in a once-daily dose of 500 mg for 1 to 3 days.

In place of Pepto-Bismol, many travelers use Imodium (loperamide hydrochloride), an over-the-counter synthetic opioid. Quinolone antibiotics such as Ciprofloxacin, ofloxacin, or levolfloxacin should be considered anytime the diarrhea is severe or associated with fever or bloody stools. Women on oral contraceptives may wish to begin taking a quinolone antibiotic for treatment of severe diarrhea sooner rather than later since severe diarrhea can cause impaired absorption of oral contraceptives. Trimethoprim-sulfamethoxazole (Bactrim, Septra) is an alternative antibiotic, but resistance has developed in many areas.

Rehydration Mix If watery diarrhea persists or is severe, and especially if the patient is vomiting and becoming dehydrated, rehydration solution should be given. It is a good idea to carry packets of ORS, such as rice-based CeraLyte (Cera Products 410–997–2334) or the older glucose-based WHO rehydration formula (Jianas Brothers— 816–421–2880). At present, many physicians specializing in travel medicine recommend the rice-based product over glucose-based ORS because studies have shown the liquid output of diarrhea is decreased in rice-based ORS and is increased in glucose-based ORS.

Rehydration mix can be made up on the spot if the prepackaged type is unavailable: to 1 quart of disinfected water add ½ teaspoon table salt (sodium chloride), ½ teaspoon baking soda (not baking powder), ¼ teaspoon potassium chloride (salt substitute), and glucose (2 to 3 tablespoons table sugar or 2 tablespoons honey or Karo syrup). Alternate with 1 quart of plain disinfected water.

Here is another simple way of preparing rehydration mix: put a 3-finger pinch of table salt in a 10-oz. glass of orange juice. Then make a little mound of table sugar in the palm of your hand and dump the sugar into the glass of orange juice. Drink this alternately with disinfected water (boil or treat with iodine). It helps to add a 3-finger pinch of baking soda (sodium bicarbonate) per 10-oz. glass to supply sodium bicarbonate, but, unless you are really going down the tubes, the baking soda is not absolutely necessary.

Avoid dairy products, as these may aggravate diarrhea in patients who are lactose intolerant.

MALARIA

I got the call from Charles' wife late one evening in February, about 8 weeks after Charles and I returned from a fantastic trek in the beautiful jungles of eastern Ecuador. "John," she said, "Charlie's in the hospital in Aspen. He's not doing well."

Dorothy summarized the details of Charles' illness: Six weeks after returning from Ecuador, he began to feel weak and developed a headache. Two days later he had a low-grade fever. When he began to cough and developed generalized muscle aching, he saw his family doctor who, appropriately enough, suspected he had a bad cold or was coming down with the flu.

After the visit to his doctor, he purchased an over-the-counter decongestant and some Advil, then flew to Mexico to take care of business interests. During a week in Mexico he continued spiking fevers, now alternating with chills, and he felt completely drained. Even though he had been on appropriate antimalarial medication while in Ecuador, it crossed his mind that malaria might be the problem. He caught a flight back to Aspen and the next day again saw his family doctor, who ordered blood smears for malaria. While he was awaiting the results of his lab tests, his condition deteriorated—he became disoriented and was too weak to walk unassisted—and he was admitted to a local hospital.

I suggested that his wife request that blood smears be sent immediately to a specialist in tropical medicine in Denver. Within 24 hours a diagnosis of *P. vivax* malaria (see below) was confirmed. Charles was immediately placed on appropriate antimalarials and made a full recovery.

There are several instructive points here. First, malaria often does not follow the cyclical fever-chills-headache scenario that most individuals, including doctors, associate with this blood-borne parasite—symptoms often exactly mimic influenza. Second, currently recommended antimalarial prophylaxis medication does *not* prevent infection by the malarial parasite (see below). Third, a delay in the diagnosis of malaria most often occurs because physicians do not ask their patients about recent travel or do not entertain a high index of suspicion for diseases acquired through travel. Actually, there is a fourth point: physicians tend to associate only *P. falciparum* malaria with severe illness; you can become sick as hell from *P. vivax*.

Because malaria is such a deadly disease, travelers to jungle regions should familiarize themselves with malaria-related health issues by accessing Travelers' Health on the CDC web site: *www.cdc.gov*. Go to "Destinations," then choose the region to be visited. The site highlights malaria risk, often by regions within each country, and lists up-to-date recommendations for chemoprophylaxis—all critically important considerations for travel.

Epidemiology

Four species of malaria parasites (*Plasmodium falciparum, Plasmodium vivax, Plasmodium malariae,* and *Plasmodium ovale*) can infect humans and cause illness. All are transmitted by the bite of infected female *Anopheles* mosquitoes; occasionally malaria is transmitted by blood transfusions, IV drug abuse, or congenitally from mother to fetus. Each year, an estimated 300 million acute episodes of illness occur, and between 2.0 and 2.5 million people die of malaria. Most of the deaths result from infection with the highly virulent *P. falciparum* species.

In the not-so-distant past, malaria was endemic in North America, Europe, and northern Asia. At present malarious areas occur in Mexico, Central and South America, the island of Hispaniola, the Middle East, sub-Saharan Africa, the Indian subcontinent, Southeast Asia, and Oceania; nearly 100 countries in all. Essentially all jungle regions of the world are areas of high risk for acquiring malaria.

Species Distribution

P. falciparum and *P. vivax* occur in tropical regions worldwide—*P. falciparum* predominates in some regions, *P. vivax* in others. *P. malariae* is encountered in a somewhat spotty distribution worldwide. *P. ovale* is rare outside West Africa.

Life Cycle of Malaria Transmission Malaria is transmitted to humans by the bite of an infected *Anopheles* mosquito. The injected parasites invade liver cells, where they multiply, rupture from the liver cells, and invade red blood cells. (In the case of *P. vivax* and *P. ovale*, but not *P. falciparum*, some of the parasites may enter a dormant phase in the liver to cause delayed attacks of malaria months or even years later.) The parasites in the red cells multiply again and rupture the red blood cells, creating the typical symptoms of an attack of malaria. Female *Anopheles* mosquitoes become infected by ingesting the blood of humans that contains sexual stages of the parasite and, after a developmental sequence in the mosquito, the stage is set for the infected mosquito to transmit malaria to another victim.

Symptoms

Malaria symptoms generally develop between 1 and 3 weeks after the bite of an infected mosquito, but the interval between the bite and the onset of symptoms may be several months (in rare instances, up to a few years). The classic symptoms of malaria consist of headache, chills, and fever, followed by profuse sweating repeated every other day or every third day in a cyclical fashion.

Often, however, malaria presents as a *flulike* illness characterized by fever, chills, severe frontal headache, muscle aches, malaise (general feelings of weakness and discomfort), and sometimes vomiting, diarrhea, and coughing. It may not resemble the cyclical triad of chills, fever, and headache most patients (and many physicians) associate with classic malaria symptoms.

Infection with *P. falciparum* can lead to life-threatening complications. When red blood cells parasitized by *P. falciparum* obstruct the microcirculation of the brain (cerebral malaria), the victim can rapidly deteriorate and exhibit symptoms ranging from subtle mental changes to seizures, coma, and death. Kidney failure is another potential complication of malaria infection.

Diagnosis

Here is the important point: suspect malaria in anyone who has traveled to a malarious area in recent months who develops headache, accompanying chills and fever, and has a flulike illness *even if that per-*

son has been on antimalarial prophylaxis. Individuals who have had mosquito bites in areas of malaria risk and develop symptoms while traveling or within a few months after returning home must consult a physician for prompt evaluation including laboratory testing.

Another critical point: many physicians who practice outside areas where tropical diseases are common, or who do not have a significant interest (and training) in travel medicine, may not be attuned to the subtleties of presentation of exotic diseases. If you are symptomatic, have recently traveled in an area where you were exposed to malaria, and your doctor resists ordering the appropriate tests to rule out malaria infection—the "I am the doctor, you are the patient" stance—get a second opinion.

Specially stained "thick" and "thin" blood smears are used to diagnose infection. The thick film detects the presence of infection; the thin film is used for the critical aspect of species differentiation. Often, doctors will order blood smears taken at 8-hour intervals because of naturally fluctuating levels of parasites in the bloodstream.

Malaria must be distinguished from influenza, typhoid fever, viral encephalitis, dengue, leptospirosis, and a variety of other causes of fever and headache.

Prevention

Preventing Mosquito Bites   A brief note: Vitamin B and ultrasound devices do *not* prevent mosquito bites.

Because *Anopheles* mosquitoes usually bite only between dusk and dawn, special efforts should be made to prevent or reduce mosquito bites during the hours of darkness.

DEET   The first line of defense against mosquito bites is to apply insect repellent to exposed skin; 15 to 30 percent DEET is the repellent of choice. Do not be tempted to use stronger formulations of DEET; high-concentration formulations may pose health hazards.

Permethrin   Permethrin (Permanone)-treated clothing, netting, and gear repels and kills mosquitoes, ticks, and other arthropods. Permethrin retains this killing effect even after repeated laundering. Studies indicate permethrin-treated clothing and gear has little potential for toxicity to humans.

Clothing   Wear long-sleeved clothing and long pants, especially when outdoors at night. Permethrin may be sprayed on clothing for additional protection against biting mosquitoes.

Mosquito Netting   Bed nets or *mosquiteros* (nets designed for use with a hammock) should be used. Netting definitely should be sprayed with permethrin. Permethrin will greatly reduce the entry of mosquitoes, even on netting that has holes in it.

Chemoprophylaxis and Treatment

Malaria vaccines are in the developmental stage and may become available in the future.

Antimalarials are effective and relatively safe when taken as directed. It must be remembered, however, that *no drug regimen currently marketed guarantees protection against malaria,* and all antimalarials have potentially serious side effects. It's worth saying again: suspect malaria in anyone who has traveled to a malarious area in recent months who develops headache, accompanying chills and fever, and has a flulike illness even if that person has been on antimalarial medication.

Note: drugs for malaria prophylaxis and treatment are constantly changing because of the development of drug resistance by the parasites and because of improvements in drug efficacy and safety. Travelers and physicians must keep abreast of these changes by consulting reliable resources such as the CDC web site (*www.cdc.gov/travel*). At present, three drugs are considered first-line choices for malaria prevention in travelers: mefloquine, doxycycline, and chloroquine. Additional drugs for this purpose include Malarone and Primaquine. The choice of which of these drugs to use depends on a number of factors including the country visited, the risk of acquiring drug-resistant *P. falciparum* malaria, any previous history of allergic reaction to the antimalarial drug of choice, and accessibility of medical care. There are additional prevention (and treatment) considerations and concerns in infants, children, and in women who are pregnant or breast-feeding.

Individuals who are exposed to malaria and develop a febrile illness or flulike illness where medical attention is not readily accessible should carry medication for presumptive self-treatment (field treatment). The choice of which drug to use for field treatment depends largely on the anticipated exposure to drug-resistant *P. falciparum.* A specialist in travel medicine can prescribe appropriate medication for field treatment—usually Fansidar, quinine plus doxycycline, or Malarone. See Elaine Jong's excellent discussion of malaria prophylaxis and field treatment cited at the end of this book.

12

WOMEN IN
THE JUNGLE

Health Issues
Pregnancy

Women adapt more easily to hot, wet environments than do men.

Mortola Buchsbaum, *Women in the Wilderness*

It's mostly good news for women travelers in the tropical rainforest.

I have yet to see a woman become incapacitated by heat illness on jungle expeditions. There are probably several reasons for this: first, there may be something inherently advantageous in women's physiology that favors rapid acclimatization to heat and humidity; second, women are less likely to adopt a macho approach to "conquering the trail" and are less likely to push themselves to the edge of physical exhaustion than men; third, in general, women tend to be more sensitive to the onset of illness and report not feeling well to associates or caregivers more readily than men, thus possibly averting a downward spiral of serious heat-related illness.

Based on my personal experiences in the jungle, women adapt to changing conditions differently and sometimes more rationally than men. It may be that women are more selective in risk-taking behaviors and thus more likely than men to say, "To hell with this, it's too dangerous." Once committed to seeing a thing through, however, it is my subjective sense that women develop strategies that favor rapid adaptation to circumstances.

HEALTH ISSUES

Women who are pregnant, breast-feeding, or traveling with small children will find authoritative recommendations on a variety of travel-related health issues at the CDC web site (*www.cdc.gov*).

Pretravel Gynecologic Exam

Women who anticipate particularly strenuous physical activity or prolonged jungle travel should schedule a pretravel gynecologic examination to detect preventable problems. A gynecologist will examine the uterus to detect the presence of fibroids, which might result in profuse bleeding, and check for ovarian cysts, which might rupture during vigorous exercise.

Sexually active women, even those using contraception, should be tested for unrecognized early pregnancy (using a pregnancy test kit), and consideration should be given to performing an ultrasound test for ectopic pregnancy. A ruptured ectopic pregnancy in a remote region away from proper medical care can result in the woman's death.

Contraception

Use only monophasic or multiphasic oral contraception pills, not progestin-only pills. See below regarding options to postpone menstruation on expeditions.

Menstruation

Many women find tampons rather than sanitary napkins more convenient for wilderness travel. Women's hygiene products should be kept dry in plastic zipper-seal bags. Used pads should be sealed in plastic bags and carried out, or buried (not sealed in bags) away from campsites.

Ibuprofen (Motrin) 600 mg taken 3 times daily can relieve severe menstrual cramps. Women who are nearly immobilized due to monthly periods should attempt to make plans to avoid travel during menstruation or consider postponing withdrawal bleeding.

Women who are taking oral contraceptives and wish to postpone withdrawal bleeding during jungle expeditions should speak with their gynecologist or family physician.

Vaginitis

Vaginal yeast infections are characterized by itching accompanied by a thick, curdy (cottage-cheese) discharge. Vaginal yeast infections respond to miconazole cream used intravaginally for three successive nights or Diflucan 150 mg as a single oral dose.

Other common causes of vaginitis, such as infection with *Gardnerella* or *Trichomonas*, are characterized by a thin, foul-smelling discharge. For these nonyeast forms of vaginitis, metronidazole (Flagyl) 250 mg taken 3 times daily for 7 days is effective.

Urinary Tract Infections

Urinary tract infections, signaled by frequency, urgency, and burning on urination, can be treated with Cipro 500 mg, one tablet twice daily for 3 days. Septra DS or Bactrim DS, one tablet twice daily for 3 days, is an alternative regimen.

Skin

Nipple irritation is fairly common in women and even men who trek long hours in the hot, humid tropics; get relief by smearing antibiotic ointment on the nipples each morning prior to trekking. Many women use snug-fitting sports bras to reduce the sensitivity of the nipples.

Scented lotions, moisturizers, and perfumes attract insects; jungle travelers must avoid looking and smelling like a flower.

Clothing

Women should wear light-colored, lightweight, full-length pants and long-sleeved shirts. Avoid floral patterns. Do not wear synthetic briefs, which trap moisture in the vaginal area; instead wear only cotton.

Privacy

In tribal villages, it is generally the custom that men bathe with men, women with women.

During menstruation, changes of tampons and pads require some provision for privacy.

Personal Safety

Leave your jewelry, especially items of gold and diamonds, at home. Wear an inexpensive wristwatch.

PREGNANCY

Although pregnant women in wilderness environments may perform as well as women in the nonpregnant state, my suggestion is that pregnant women with the urge to participate in a wilderness experience restrict their travel to temperate climates. If, despite the risks involved, pregnant women choose to take part in a wilderness jungle experience, travel should be limited to areas where malaria is not endemic and where there is prompt and reliable transportation to expert medical care.

The American College of Obstetricians and Gynecologists recommends the second trimester (18 to 24 weeks) as the safest time for travel by pregnant women. First trimester pregnancies carry a significant risk of miscarriage and third trimester pregnancies put women at increased risk for premature labor, preterm rupture of membranes, and other problems.

13

TRAVELING WITH CHILDREN IN THE TROPICS

Guidelines for Traveling with
    Children
Special Pediatric Health
    Concerns
Pediatric Medical Kit

Does one ever see things clearer than as a child?

Ludwig Bemelmans

The extra demands on parents and the risks inherent in traveling with infants and small children (under age 6) in *remote* jungle regions probably outweigh potential rewards. But a stay at a "jungle lodge" oriented toward ecotourism and catering to families, however, can prove ideal for children of any age. There are a number of such facilities in Costa Rica's splendid Corcovado National Park.

GUIDELINES FOR TRAVELING WITH CHILDREN

The following general guidelines must be considered when traveling with children in the tropical forest:

1. *Duration of jungle trek* Do not attempt a day-long hike. Indigenous children can hike all day in the humid tropical forest; an unacclimated, nonnative child cannot. In the jungle, a hike of 1 to 2 hours is plenty for the preadolescent, or 2 to 4

hours of strenuous trekking (up and down hills, for example) for children aged 12 to 16.

2. *Terrain*   Do not attempt difficult or dangerous trails. Do not subject a child to arduous jungle trail conditions unless the child has had extensive experience hiking in temperate climates.

3. *Season*   Avoid trekking during the rainy season.

4. *Fluid and electrolyte replacement*   Children acclimate to hot environments at a slower rate than adults. Keep the child well hydrated. Although children sweat less than adults and have a lower concentration of salt in their sweat, they can still get in trouble fast from fluid and electrolyte loss. Before hitting the trail, load your child up on fluids with about ¼ to ½ packet of oral rehydration mixture added; ½ hour later the child should consume more water; 1 hour later still more water; 1 to 2 hours later more water. Children usually will not drink extra fluids on their own unless actively encouraged.

5. *Footwear*   Provide proper footwear (running or hiking shoes with an adequate tread). Avoid all-leather boots.

6. *Children should be seen at all times*   Children should not be out of sight on the trail. Keep the child ahead of you and behind a native guide. Children must be taught to stay put if they stray off the trail. Children old enough to wander off on their own should carry an orange whistle capable of emitting a loud sound. (Three blasts—"Help! I'm lost!" Two blasts—"We hear you. We're coming.") Practice "what to do when lost in the woods" at home before venturing into the jungle; it is not enough to *tell* a child what to do—you must practice the drill.

   Any pack carried by a child should have red-orange and silver reflective patches sewn on it. Consideration should be given to sewing reflective material on all outer garments worn by children or have the child wear a lightweight, brightly colored (red-orange) shirt.

7. *Water safety*   When wading across rivers, have an adult native guide hold the child's hand. *Always* have children wear a properly sized life vest while rafting, taking canoe trips, or crossing deep, swift, or wide rivers.

A special word of caution regarding swimming: any child who plans to visit the tropics should be a strong swimmer. Many natives begin swimming in infancy and are accustomed to bathing and playing in deep or rapidly flowing water that would be extremely hazardous to visiting children. Swimming holes are often located in the swift-flowing outer loop of jungle rivers where depths plunge suddenly to 6 feet or more within a yard of the shoreline.

8. *Gear* Do not allow a small child to carry any equipment in a daypack other than two bottles of drinking water. Adolescents can carry personal drinking water plus snacks and a lightweight point-and-shoot camera.

SPECIAL PEDIATRIC HEALTH CONCERNS

Always arrange a pretrip visit with a family physician, pediatrician, or physician specializing in the specialty of travel medicine before traveling with children in jungle regions.

Medication

The dose of medication (snake antivenin excepted—see below) should be calculated based on the weight of the child.

Overdose of antimalarial drugs can be *fatal*. Medication should be stored in *childproof containers* out of reach of children.

Traveler's Diarrhea in Children

The greatest risk to infants and small children who acquire travelers' diarrhea is dehydration. Oral Rehydration Solution (ORS) packets are sold in stores and pharmacies in most developing countries and should be carried at all times by parents who travel with small children. Breast-fed infants with diarrhea should continue nursing on demand.

Vaccinations

Parents should check with their pediatrician or family physician to make sure a child's routine vaccinations are up to date before traveling to third-world countries.

Special vaccinations such as yellow fever and typhoid should be considered for certain jungle areas. Hepatitis A vaccine is recommended. Although children who are infected with hepatitis A generally have a subclinical disease (manifest few if any symptoms), asymptomatic hepatitis A-infected children shed virus in their stool and are a threat to nonimmune adults.

Detailed advice on vaccinations for children is available from the Centers for Disease Control (*www.cdc.gov*). The frequently updated publication, *Health Information for International Travel* (for sale by the Superintendent of Documents, U.S. Government Printing Office, Washington, D.C., 20402) contains an excellent, authoritative section on vaccine recommendations for children traveling abroad. This is the same information that is available on the CDC web site.

Envenomation

Snakes, spiders, and scorpions deliver the same dose of venom irrespective of the size of the victim. Because of the increased dose of venom per pound of weight, small children often experience greater toxic effects from envenomation.

A common therapeutic error in treating snake envenomation is to give a child a lesser amount of antivenin. With respect to snakebite, it is critical to keep in mind that children may require larger doses per unit of body weight than do adults.

Ectoparasites

In some villages, scabies and head lice are present in nearly 100 percent of the population. Children, with their tendency to make close personal contact and exchange clothing and head gear, are primed for infestation.

Scabies is a parasitic skin disease caused by a mite, *Sarcoptes scabiei*. The patient is aggravated by intense itching, especially at night. Generally several family members are infected. The condition may be diagnosed by finding raised lesions (papules and vesicles) and tiny linear burrows on the fingers, finger webs, and genitalia. Elimite (5 percent permethrin) generally is effective. Older topical preparations such as lindane, benzylbenzoate, and 10 percent crotamiton are also effective. All affected family members should be treated simultaneously. Pregnant and lactating females should avoid using lindane. It is helpful to thoroughly wash clothing and bed linens in hot water following treatment.

The head louse, *Pediculus humanus capitus*, is worldwide in distribution. Children generally complain of an itchy scalp, particularly in the region at the back of the neck and near the ears. Head lice (3 mm long) are fast moving and difficult to detect. Their eggs ("nits"), though small, are quite distinctive, and will be found firmly cemented to a hair shaft. Unlike dandruff, they cannot be flicked off. Head lice may be treated with 1 percent permethrin (Nix) or 0.5 percent malathion.

Insect Repellant

Despite previously reported concerns, there is no firm evidence that the concentration of DEET found in insect repellants such as *OFF!* is harmful to children *when applied properly.* Spray lightly; do not saturate the skin. There is plenty of evidence that diseases carried by mosquitoes can harm and kill children. Use DEET!

Sun Protection

Children exposed to harsh tropical sun should always wear a hat and UV-protective clothing, and they should lather up with sunblock with SPF of at least 15.

PEDIATRIC MEDICAL KIT

Drs. Eric A. Weiss and Barbara Kennedy, who know a thing or two about medical needs in the wilderness setting, have designed the Family Spirit Kit, which will help you prevent, evaluate, and treat injuries and illnesses in infants, children, and adults. Chinook Medical Gear, Inc. (*www.chinookmed.com*) and Travel Medicine, Inc. (*www.travmed.com*) stock the Family Spirit Kit and other kits designed for the first aid needs of children.

14

INFECTIOUS DISEASES

Bacterial Infections
Viral Infections
Parasitic Diseases

A comprehensive discussion of the vast array of infectious diseases in the tropics is beyond the scope of this work, which is designed primarily as a portable guide for the nonphysician. Readers who have no formal training in the medical specialties will benefit from the discussions of common bacterial, viral, and parasitic diseases in Stuart R. Rose's frequently updated *International Travel Health Guide* referenced at the end of this book. Readers with a medical background will find the references for Cook and Strickland, also at the end of this book, of particular interest with respect to in-depth discussion of both common and rare tropical diseases.

BACTERIAL ILLNESSES

Tuberculosis

Quick Reference

- Chronic cough, often with blood-tinged sputum

- Fever, night sweats, weight loss, and easy fatigability

- Typical findings on chest X ray

- Positive tuberculin skin test

- Acid-fast bacilli on sputum smear and in culture

- Multiple-drug treatment is effective

In 1968, while living with Chachi Indians in the lush tropical forest of the Cayapa River Basin in Ecuador, I first became aware of the extent of morbidity and mortality secondary to tuberculosis. It was common to encounter individuals with a chronic cough, blood-tinged sputum, weight loss, and night sweats. It was disturbingly routine to enter a hut and find an emaciated victim of tuberculosis lying in a far corner, awaiting death. During that era, one could hardly spend a week on the river without passing a canoe of mourners who were on their way to or returning from a funeral.

Epidemiology Tuberculosis of the lungs is, unfortunately, still very common throughout the poorer nations of the world. Although impressive results in the control of tuberculosis have been achieved in the technically advanced countries, there has been little or no improvement in most countries in the tropics, where an estimated 85 percent of the world's tuberculosis now occurs. Approximately 10 million people develop tuberculosis disease in poor countries each year and at least 3 million die of the disease. Even in the United States, over 20,000 cases are reported annually.

The infectious agent, *Mycobacterium tuberculosis,* is transmitted from person to person by exposure to airborne droplets when patients having active disease cough or sneeze. Generally, though not always, persons at highest risk of acquiring infection with the tubercle bacilli are close contacts—those living in the same household with the infectious case, close friends, or fellow workers. The disease may occasionally be spread by the ingestion of raw unpasteurized milk or other dairy products. Worldwide, about 10 percent of *infected* persons ultimately develop clinically *active* tuberculosis.

Clinical Manifestations Tuberculosis should be suspected in individuals who have a chronic cough *lasting more than several weeks,* fever, chills, night sweats, easy fatigability, and weight loss. One should be especially suspicious if the patient coughs up blood-tinged sputum.

Although tuberculosis occurs most commonly as an infection of the lungs, other sites within the body may be involved, including the meninges, lymph nodes, kidneys, bones, skin, and intestines.

Diagnosis One may get clues that aid in the diagnosis of tuberculosis disease by performing the tuberculin skin test and by chest X ray. The tuberculin skin test does not distinguish between current disease and past infection; it only indicates that the individual has been infected at some time with the bacterium. Therefore, a positive tuberculin skin test does *not* prove that a person has *active* disease. The chest X ray, while suggestive of disease, is not *proof* of disease. Any number of other conditions including parasitic lung-fluke disease (paragonimiasis) and the fungal disease histoplasmosis may simulate the appearance of tuberculosis on chest X ray.

Diagnosis is made by detecting the organism in stained smears of sputum and by recovery of *M. tuberculosis* from cultures or identification of the organism by DNA probe.

Treatment A number of drugs are used currently to treat pulmonary tuberculosis, including isoniazid, rifampin, pyrazinamide, streptomycin, and ethambutol. In the United States, an initial four-drug regimen usually is recommended.

Tuberculin Skin Test If you have not had a tuberculin skin test in several years and if your last test was known to be negative, it would be a good idea to get a skin test *prior* to traveling to an area where there is a high prevalence of tuberculosis. You should receive the standard Mantoux test (an intradermal injection of 0.1 mL of PPD tuberculin) and not the multiple puncture "tine" test. Two to three months after you return from your trip, especially if you develop symptoms, get another Mantoux text. If positive, there is a strong likelihood that you have had recent infection by *M. tuberculosis*. Recent conversion from negative to positive generally requires preventive therapy using the drug isoniazid. Interpretation of the tuberculin skin test is not as straightforward as once thought. The "boosting" phenomenon can give a false impression of conversion and there are numerous reasons why false-positive and false-negative tuberculin reactions may occur.

Two points about tuberculin skin testing: 1) Absence of a reaction to the tuberculin skin test does not exclude the diagnosis of tuberculosis. The response to the test may be decreased in persons with any severe or febrile illness, measles, HIV infection (AIDS), live-virus vaccination, Hodgkin's disease, after the administration of corticosteroids or immunosuppressive drugs, and, curiously, in patients with overwhelming disease due to tuberculosis. 2) In the past, it was thought individuals with previous BCG vaccination (see below) generally have a positive reaction to tuberculin skin testing, making the skin test unreliable. Althought the tuberculin skin test may be positive for approximately 1 year after BCG vaccination, current guidelines advise that interpretation of the skin test does not change because of suspected or known vaccination with BCG.

Prevention Recent tuberculin skin-test converters are candidates for preventive therapy using the drug isoniazid to substantially reduce the risk of developing clinically active tuberculosis.

Live tuberculosis vaccines, known collectively as BCG, are available. In selected third-world populations, BCG appears to have had a significant impact on reducing the number of new cases of tuberculosis. Case-control studies consistently demonstrate protection against tuberculosis meningitis and disseminated disease in children less than 5 years old.

So, why isn't BCG vaccine used routinely for travel in regions where the prevalence of tuberculosis is high? First, there is currently no way to know if any given batch of vaccine is effective or not! That is to say, some batches of newly manufactured vaccine seem to be reasonably effective (up to 76 percent) while others are essentially worthless. This variable effectiveness has never been adequately explained. Neither the *Medical Letter on Drugs and Therapeutics* in its "Advice For Travelers" issue nor the Centers for Disease Control and Prevention (CDC) recommends routine use of BCG vaccine for travelers. By current guidelines, BCG vaccine may, however, be *considered* for tuberculin-negative persons, especially children, who are repeatedly exposed to individuals with untreated or ineffectively treated tuberculosis and who cannot receive standard isoniazid preventive therapy.

Should jungle trekkers consider BCG vaccine? Probably not. Because you are unlikely to contract tuberculosis in your wanderings and because there is no way to determine whether or not the dose of vaccine you receive will be from a "good" batch or a "bad" batch, it seems reasonable, at this time, not to take BCG vaccine. In addition, recent BCG immunization may cause a positive reaction to the tuberculin skin test, thus complicating decisions about prescribing treatment for infection.

On the other hand, if you plan to work with or live intimately with populations where tuberculosis is rampant, you might want to think about BCG vaccine. It is best to check with a physician specializing in travel medicine who is well versed on the pros and cons of BCG vaccination.

Typhoid Fever

Quick Reference

- An acute, life-threatening illness caused by the bacterium *Salmonella* serotype *typhi.*

- Gradual onset of slowly rising temperature (over a period of days), general malaise, headache, sore throat, cough, and "pea soup" diarrhea (or constipation). "Rose" spots. Slow pulse for the amount of fever. Distended and tender abdomen.

- Diagnosis by blood, urine, and stool culture for *Salmonella typhi.* Serologic tests aid in diagnosis.

- Treatment using Cipro or alternative drugs including ampicillin, chloramphenicol, and trimethoprim-sulfamethoxazole.

- Vaccines protect 50 to 80 percent of recipients.

Epidemiology Typhoid fever is caused by infection with the typhoid bacillus, *Salmonella typhi.* It is transmitted by food or water that has been contaminated by feces or urine of patients or carriers. Shellfish may be a source of infection.

Typhoid fever is found throughout the world, especially in poorer nations where health standards may be lax.

Clinical Manifestations Classically there are three recognized stages:

I. After infecting the intestinal wall, the bacteria spread to various organs in the body, causing fever, headache, sore throat, cough, general body aching, and nosebleeds. In addition, patients complain of abdominal pain, diarrhea or constipation, and vomiting.

II. After a week or 10 days the fever, which up to this point has risen in a "step-wise" fashion, stabilizes and the patients become very ill and develop "pea-soup" diarrhea (occasionally constipation) with marked distension of the abdomen. During this phase patients often develop "rose" spots. This rash is characterized by the appearance of little pink raised spots, mainly on the trunk, which fade when pressure is applied. The rash of typhoid fever generally lasts 3 to 4 days. In this stage patients look very ill, yet the pulse is lower than might be expected.

III. Those untreated patients who survive enter a stage of clinical improvement with declining fever, decreased abdominal symptoms, and increasing alertness.

Diagnosis *S. typhi* can be cultured from the blood, stool, and urine. Serologic tests are available to aid in the diagnosis.

Treatment Since 10 percent of patients with untreated disease die, hospitalization and rapid diagnosis are essential. Patients may be treated with ampicillin, chloramphenicol, trimethoprim-sulfamethoxazole (Bactrim or Septra) or Cipro (ciprofloxacin). The unvaccinated trekker who comes down with symptoms of typhoid fever should start Cipro, 500 mg or 750 mg twice daily for 10 days if medical facilities are not close by.

Prevention   Travelers to jungle regions of Africa, Asia, and Central and South America should be protected against typhoid fever. Of the three typhoid vaccines currently available in the United States, choose *either* the oral live-attenuated vaccine Ty21a (Vivotif Berna) or the capsular polysaccharide vaccine for injection (Typhim Vi). A booster dose of the oral live-attenuated Ty21a vaccine should be given every 5 years; a booster injection of Vi capsular polysaccharide vaccine is recommended every 2 years. All typhoid vaccines protect between 50 and 80 percent of recipients.

Shigellosis (Bacillary Dysentery)

Quick Reference

- Watery diarrhea, often with blood and mucus.

- Fever, chills, abdominal pain, headache, malaise.

- Patients experience pain and strain as they pass small-volume stool.

- White blood cells in stools. Stool culture.

- Treatment with trimethoprim-sulfamethoxazole or ciprofloxacin.

Epidemiology   Shigellosis, also known as bacillary dysentery, is caused by infection with any of four species of *Shigella*. This bacterial disease is encountered worldwide and is endemic in the tropics. The only significant reservoir is humans. Transmission is fecal-oral, either directly from infected individuals who do not wash their hands, or from contaminated food or water. Flies can transfer the infectious organisms.

Clinical Manifestations   The onset of symptoms is often abrupt with fever, sometimes chills, abdominal pain, and dysentery (diarrheal stool containing mucus and blood). These patients may experience intense straining from the urge to defecate, often without results. Patients with common travelers' diarrhea due to *E. coli* often joke between bouts of diarrhea; those with dysentery due to *Shigella* are too sick to see any humor in the situation. These patients are "toxic"—they look and feel like hell. About 3 percent of patients infected with *Shigella flexneri* will develop joint pains, irritation of the eyes, and pain on urination: a condition known as Reiter's syndrome.

Diagnosis   Microscopic examination of the stool reveals white cells and red cells. The stool culture is usually positive.

Treatment   Many specialists recommend trimethoprim-sulfame-thoxazole (Bactrim or Septra) double-strength, one tablet twice daily for 3 days or ciprofloxacin 500 mg every 12 hours for 3 doses.

Prevention   Drink only boiled or treated water. Eat only cooked, hot foods. Peel all fruit yourself.

Leptospirosis

Epidemiology   Leptospirosis is a zoonosis that is endemic in the tropics and infects a number of domestic and wild animals, particularly rats. The infectious agent is a leptospire that is excreted in the urine of carrier animals. Humans become infected when the leptospires enter via the conjunctiva or through breaks in the skin. On occasion, transmission may occur through ingestion of food contaminated with the urine of infected rats. Cases have been associated with canoeing, kayaking, and swimming in contaminated lakes and rivers. Outbreaks are especially common after heavy rains when flooding facilitates the spread of leptospires present in the soil.

Clinical Manifestations   These patients present with an abrupt onset of fever, muscle aches (especially the calf muscles), and headache. It is the *sudden onset of intense frontal headache* that is so characteristic of this illness: patients can often tell you to the exact minute when the headache had its onset. The headache does not build up; one minute it is not there, the next—bang!—the patient is reeling in pain. The eyes are bloodshot. Another characteristic, not given much attention in medical literature, is the sometimes subtle personality changes the victims exhibit. The fever comes in phases: initially there is a dramatic, abrupt temperature elevation, then after a few days a period of improvement in symptoms and lowering or absence of fever, followed by a recurrence of symptoms including a persistent high fever. Some patients experience a rash.

A severe form of leptospirosis, usually caused by *Leptospira icterohaemorrhagiae,* is characterized by jaundice (yellowing of the skin and conjunctivae), kidney failure, impaired liver function, hemorrhage, and shock. The mortality rate in patients with jaundice is approximately 5 percent for children and young adults and as high as 30 percent for those over age 60.

Diagnosis   Diagnosis is made by serologic tests and by isolation of leptospires from the blood and cerebral spinal fluid in the first week of illness or from the urine after the tenth day of illness.

Treatment   A number of drugs, including penicillin and doxycycline, have been used to treat this condition.

Prevention   There is no practical means of preventing this un-common infection.

VIRAL INFECTIONS

A hodgepodge of viral illnesses exist in the tropics, many of which can be quite debilitating, even fatal. To cover more than a frac-tion of the potential viral illnesses infecting man is beyond the scope of this book: among the arboviruses alone, some 90 different agents cause disease in man! Travelers in the tropics should be aware of the following viral infections:

Dengue (Breakbone Fever)

Quick Reference

- Sudden onset of high fever, severe aching, headache, sore throat. Patients feel like bones are "breaking."

- Rash that begins on hands and feet and spreads to torso. Rash has onset 3 or 4 days into illness, often during a temporary re-mission of fever.

- Dengue Hemorrhagic Fever, a more serious form of disease, causes bleeding of the gastrointestinal tract, shock and, often, death.

- No antibiotics or vaccine available for prevention or treatment.

- Prevent by using DEET and mosquito netting.

Epidemiology   This virus is transmitted by the mostly day-biting *Aedes aegypti* mosquito. Disease occurs in tropical regions of Asia, the Pacific Islands, northern Queensland Australia, tropical Africa, Cen-tral and South America, and the Caribbean. Dengue fever occurs en-demically and as periodic epidemics and is found in both rural and urban areas; the risk is often highest in urban areas.

Clinical Manifestations   Illness begins with the sudden onset of high fever, chills, and severe aching ("breakbone") of the head, back, arms, and legs. There is usually an accompanying sore throat, redness of the eyes, and a blotchy skin rash that comes on 3 to 4 days after the onset of illness. The rash usually appears first on the back of the hands and feet and then spreads to the arms, legs, and trunk. The rash lasts hours to days and may be followed by desquamation (peeling) of the skin. From a diagnostic standpoint, it is significant that the rash usu-ally spares the face. Recovery is characterized by prolonged feelings of fatigue and depression.

A more severe form of illness, Dengue Hemorrhagic Fever, occurs sporadically throughout the world (particularly in Asia, the Caribbean, Mexico, and Central America) and is characterized initially by the typical symptoms and signs of the more benign form of dengue. These patients eventually develop bleeding from the nose, gums, and gastrointestinal tract, and may go into shock and die.

Diagnosis   Infection is diagnosed by a blood test.

Treatment   Treatment is supportive only: bed rest, fluids, and acetaminophen to reduce fever. Do not give aspirin to patients with this febrile illness. Patients with hemorrhagic illness require hospitalization in anticipation of treatment for shock.

Prevention   No vaccine is available for dengue fever. DEET insect repellent should be used, especially during the daytime, and mosquito nets should be used at night.

Yellow Fever

Quick Reference

- Sudden onset of severe headache, pain behind the eyes, nausea, vomiting. As the fever rises, the heart rate decreases.

- Yellow skin and eyes. "Coffee-ground" vomitus. Bleeding into the skin and gastrointestinal tract.

- Diagnosis: decreased white cell count; increased bilirubin in blood and urine; serologic tests.

- Treatment: no specific treatment.

- Prevention: safe and highly effective yellow fever vaccine available.

Epidemiology   Yellow fever currently occurs only in Africa and South America and is transmitted by *Aedes* or forest mosquitoes. (Historically, yellow fever was found as far north as Philadelphia and Baltimore in the United States.) There are two transmission cycles, urban and jungle. The urban cycle involves humans and mosquitoes. Jungle disease is maintained by mosquitoes and nonhuman primates with occasional transmission to humans by infectious mosquitoes.

Clinical Manifestations   Like dengue fever, yellow fever is characterized by the sudden onset of severe headache and aching of the legs and back. There is accompanying fever, nausea, and vomiting. The pulse may be slow and weak, out of proportion to the fever. Jaundice (yellowing of the skin and eyes) usually occurs early in the course of the disease.

Some cases progress to a more severe form, often after a brief remission of hours to a day or two. The severe form of yellow fever is characterized by slowed heart rate, nosebleeds, bleeding of the gums, copious black vomitus, blood in the stool, decreased or absent urination, and intractable hiccups. Mortality is high in severe disease, with death occurring between the sixth and tenth days.

Diagnosis   Serologic tests establish the diagnosis. Other clues include a low white cell count, abnormal liver function tests, and protein in the urine.

Treatment   There is no specific treatment.

Prevention   Travelers to areas of South America and Africa where yellow fever is known to occur should receive Yellow Fever Vaccine. This live-virus vaccine is safe and highly effective. Some countries require a valid yellow fever vaccination card before entry at the border.

Viral Hemorrhagic Fevers

Ebola kills a great deal of tissue while the host is still alive. It triggers a creeping, spotty necrosis that spreads through all the internal organs. The liver bulges up and turns yellow, begins to liquefy, and then it cracks apart.

Richard Preston, *Hot Zone*

A large number of viruses, collectively known as the hemorrhagic fevers, cause illness in man. These truly exotic diseases are the stuff of nightmares and horror movies.

Epidemiology   The hemorrhagic fever viruses are grouped into four distinct families and share these features: all are RNA viruses; their survival is dependent on an animal or insect host (natural reservoir); the viruses are geographically restricted; humans are not the natural reservoir for any of these viruses, although with some, once infected, humans can transmit the virus to another person; outbreaks occur sporadically and thus cannot be predicted; with few exceptions, there is no cure or proven drug treatment.

The zoonotic viruses, which naturally reside in an animal reservoir (usually rodents) or arthropod vectors, include Junin hemorrhagic fever and Machupo hemorrhagic fever in South America, hantavirus pulmonary syndrome in South America, and Lassa fever in

West Africa. Although both Marburg and Ebola viruses appear to be zoonotic infections, the natural reservoirs remain undetermined.

Clinical Manifestations Victims of viral hemorrhagic fever illnesses generally manifest signs and symptoms that include marked fever, fatigue, muscle aches, altered mental status, and in severe cases signs of bleeding under the skin and from body orifices. Ebola Hemorrhagic Fever of central Africa, famed for its horrific tendency to essentially *liquefy* all organs in the human body, gained much publicity through Richard Preston's article "Crisis in the Hot Zone," which appeared in *The New Yorker* and in his critically acclaimed book *The Hot Zone.*

Diagnosis and Case Management Early diagnosis, usually made by virus isolation or ELISA testing, is important because some of these deadly infections are highly transmissible to close contacts, making **patient isolation** a critical step in interrupting the spread of disease. Blood, body secretions, and tissue suspected of harboring the most highly pathogenic viruses are handled in special facilities such as the Special Pathogens Branch (BSL4 laboratory) at the CDC. The antiviral drug, ribavirin, has been effective in treating some patients with Lassa fever; for most of the other entities, there is no specific treatment.

Reality Check The prospect of lethal viral diseases that have been living undetected in jungle regions, perhaps for eons, entering human populations is real, but, AIDS aside, exceptionally uncommon. It is very unlikely the jungle traveler will succumb to any of these gruesome entities; you have a much higher chance of coming to an untimely end as a result of a careless driver running a red light within a block or two of your own home.

PARASITIC DISEASES

Travelers are at risk for any number of parasitic diseases that are encountered throughout the tropics. Fortunately, the risk of acquiring the insect-borne diseases such as malaria, filariasis (the cause of disfiguring elephantiasis), leishmaniasis (ulcerating lesions of the skin and mucous membranes), and River Blindness (onchocerciasis) can be greatly reduced by the use of DEET containing insect repellents on the skin and the pretreatment of clothing with permethrin.

Water- and food-borne diseases such as ascariasis (roundworm), trichuriasis (whipworm), trichinosis, paragonimiasis (lung fluke), and the protozoan intestinal parasites (amebiasis, giardiasis, cryptosporidiosis, and cyclosporiasis) are best avoided by following the recommendations given elsewhere in this book regarding safe drinking water and the proper preparation of food. Parasites such as hookworm and strongyloidiasis, which gain entry into the human host through penetration of the skin (usually the soles of the feet), can be prevented by avoiding walking around barefoot—always wear shoes in the tropics!

15

SURVIVAL STRATEGIES

Basic Strategies to Improve
  Rescue and Survival Odds
When Rescue Is Not Feasible:
  Getting Out on Your Own
Potable Water
Finding Food
Emergency Shelter
Making Fire
Making Cooking Utensils
Psychology of Survival
Strategies to Increase Survivor
  Confidence

The focus of survival in the jungle should be geared toward efforts that will get the traveler out—fast.

BASIC STRATEGIES TO IMPROVE RESCUE AND SURVIVAL ODDS

Every year, inexperienced people enter the jungle and get lost. After a person ventures but a few yards into the forest, especially jungle that has been cleared and is now a tangle of secondary growth, everything begins to look the same.

To avoid getting lost, travelers should always have an experienced guide when traversing unfamiliar territory. People, particularly indigenous tribesmen, reared in the tropical forest have an uncanny ability to find their way and arrive at the desired destination even after days of travel. They can always find food and water and, if necessary, rapidly construct a shelter or a weapon from the bountiful forest.

For individuals unfortunate enough to be in a survival situation in the jungle, an unbeatable combination of potentially lifesaving items includes a large-scale map, a global positioning system (GPS) unit, some form of lightweight electronic voice communication, a butane lighter, small strips of rubber tire, Potable Aqua tablets, and, above all, a machete. Reduced to bare essentials, always travel with a machete, butane lighter, and Potable Aqua tablets.

Maps and Satellite Images

Detailed, laminated maps (where available) should always be carried for any area to be traversed. Topographic maps are available from numerous international and national mapping agencies. Satellite images with extraordinary resolution are available from Space Imaging, 800–232–9307, *www.spaceimaging.com* or from Customer Services, U.S. Geological Survey, Eros Data Center, 800–252–4547, *edcwww.cr.usgs.gov.*

GPS

Lightweight global position system (GPS) units are the size of a paperback novel, cheap, and display precise latitude, longitude, and, often, altitude. The Garmin eTrex, a 12 parallel channel GPS receiver, is incredibly compact (2" × 4.4" × 1.2"), lightweight (5.3 oz), and waterproof (30 min @ 1m), but does not display altitude. It has a unique TrackBack feature that plots your return route without entering waypoints on the outbound leg. The new, more expensive Garmin eTrex Summit is a combination GPS, altimeter, and electronic compass.

The information available from GPS units is extremely useful for navigation and for communicating one's position to rescue aircraft. When used in clearings or in open areas along a river, GPS receivers quickly lock onto satellites and display information. For emergency use, the newer units are more likely to work under the jungle canopy than earlier versions.

Satellite Phone

Handheld satellite phones are available for communication over most of the world. Although currently expensive to purchase and operate, their potential to provide would-be rescuers with details of the emergency and precise GPS location make these lightweight phones worthy of serious consideration for inclusion in high-risk wilderness expeditions. Over the next few years it is reasonable to anticipate a dramatic drop in the initial purchase price and per-minute rates of satellite phone service.

EPIRB/Personal Locator Beacon

Canoeists or rafters contemplating an expedition into largely un-inhabited and unexplored regions should consider buying a compact emergency position-indicating radio beacon (EPIRB). The new 406 MHZ EPIRB units offer a reliable method of alerting rescue services via a global satellite system. These units should be activated only in a true emergency when lives are at risk. Overland expeditioners should consider ACR electronics (*www.acrelectronics.com*) GyPSI™ 406 Personal Locator Beacon. This small (1.9 × 6.5 × 3.8 inches), lightweight (17.6 ounce) unit can be carried in a pack and has a waterproof GPS and programming interface to transmit GPS data for even faster response.

Rescue by Aircraft

VHF Transceiver Lightweight, handheld aircraft VHF band transceivers are excellent for emergency communications. Visitors to remote areas should *ascertain beforehand the radio frequencies that potential rescue aircraft might use*. The international aviation emergency frequency is 121.5 MHZ.

VHF transceivers are line-of-sight instruments, so they are most useful when aircraft are overhead without objects such as trees or mountains between the handheld unit and the aircraft. Do *not* point the transceiver antenna directly at the rescue aircraft; this degrades the signal appreciably. Keep the radio antenna at a right angle to the path of the rescue aircraft.

Mirror Signaling Device U.S. Air Force search-and-rescue experts consider the signal mirror the most valuable daytime means of visual signaling, even on cloudy days. According to an Air Force survival manual, a mirror flash can be visible up to 100 miles under ideal conditions! Manufactured signal mirrors incorporate an aim indicator and have instructions printed on the back of the mirror. Such devices are highly resistant to breaking and make excellent mirrors for shaving.

Improvised signal mirrors may be made from parts of downed aircraft, polished aluminum, or foil from rations. All forms of mirror signals are limited to cleared areas such as village compounds or along rivers and are useless under the jungle canopy.

Smoke and Flares Smoke from commercial, handheld smoke bombs or smoke grenades is an excellent daytime visual signal when the survivor can see the aircraft and has established voice communication with the pilot via a radio link. The pilot will give the command to "pop your smoke" and look to see where the smoke is coming from.

There are a number of commercial signal flares on the market, including those manufactured by Orion. It is usually pointless to shoot a flare during the daytime unless 1) you can see the rescue aircraft, 2) the aircraft is relatively nearby, and 3) the aircraft is heading your way. Pilots cannot see behind their aircraft and will miss spotting the flare unless it is in their line of vision.

Smoke and flares should be used out in the open: it is difficult to shoot a flare through the branches and leaves of the trees and smoke is held up by the canopy and cannot rise.

In a pinch, a pengun flare (a common handheld flare device) makes a decent short-range, one-shot weapon.

Jungle Airstrips and Landing Pads In many isolated regions of the tropics, the Mission Aviation Fellowship (MAF) or New Tribes Missions (NTM) provide air service for missionaries and natives into remote airstrips in small indigenous villages. Both MAF and NTM use grass airstrips suitable for short take-off and landing (STOL), fixed-wing aircraft. Petroleum companies often have clearings, scattered across vast areas of remote jungle, which are suitable for landing helicopters. If assistance is needed in an emergency, a handheld radio transmitter can be used to call pilots of STOL aircraft or helicopters.

Assessing Suitability of Airstrips for Landing and Take-off Bush pilots, using conventional or STOL aircraft, appreciate having information on the condition of seldom-used airstrips. Here's how to make and use a crude but acceptable device for measuring airstrip hardness: Cut a pole exactly 2 inches in diameter and approximately 6 feet long. Starting exactly 6 inches from one end, taper that end to a point. Lash a cross-member on the pole and have a person weighing approximately 170 pounds stand with assistance on the cross-member. Make a map of the strip, noting the depth to which the pointed end of the pole sinks into the earth at several dozen sites. Communicate this information to the pilot by radio. If the pole goes in only 2 inches or less in most areas, the strip is considered ideal; 2 to 4 inches is marginal; penetration beyond 4 inches indicates that the airstrip is unsuitable for landing and take-off.

Smoke from fire also gives pilots a good sense of the direction and speed of wind.

Helicopter Extraction If the helicopter is able to actually land in a rescue operation, follow the instructions of the rescue crew and approach the helicopter only from the front and sides in the 3 o'clock to 9 o'clock position relative to the nose of the aircraft. *Never* approach the helicopter from the danger zone at the rear of the aircraft in the vicinity of the tail rotor. If the helicopter has landed in an area next to a steep slope or is hovering with just one skid barely touching a sloping hill, always approach from the downhill side, *never* from the uphill side.

Various pickup devices have been employed to effect helicopter rescue on land or at sea. There are two important points to keep in mind in any emergency helicopter rescue: 1) the pickup device and drop cable must be allowed to *touch the ground or water* to lose its enormous charge of static electricity before survivors attempt to grab hold of the rescue device and 2) survivors must *follow all instructions* provided by the rescue crew. When lifted to the door of the helicopter, survivors must not attempt to grab the door or assist the hoist operator in any way.

In areas where military helicopters operate, emergency rescue of a severely injured person may involve use of the *forest penetrator,* a rescue seat that is designed to make its way through dense jungle growth; more commonly, helicopter rescue will involve other devices such as the Motley and McGuire rigs, the Swiss Seat and Stabo rig or the rope ladder.

WHEN RESCUE IS NOT FEASIBLE: GETTING OUT ON YOUR OWN

If rescue is not feasible, the traveler should continually move downstream at a fast pace.

Using Existing Trails

In inhabited areas there is usually a trail running alongside a stream. From time to time the trail may veer away from the stream where natives have cut a path to connect two villages by the shortest distance rather than following the meandering course of the river. Marking the trail every 10 yards with a machete makes it easier to return to the starting point. To avoid confusion, the traveler should mark trees only on one side of the trail.

Identification of Trails Used by Humans

Where human paths are in frequent use, identifying a trail is fairly easy. Seldom-used trails or any trail traversed during times of maximal plant growth may be extremely difficult to identify and follow for the nonnative. Even under less than ideal circumstances, however, there are clues to trail identification. Paradoxically, concentrating only on the actual footpath will almost certainly cause you to lose sight of the trail. You must learn to focus farther out than the area immediately before you and scan for unnatural breaks in the jungle foliage; learn to look *through* the jungle, not at it. Also, it is helpful to think of the jungle trail not as a track on the ground, but as the intestinal canal of "some gigantic leafy creature." Viewed in this fashion, there are vertical margins, often an overhead horizontal boundary and, sometimes, with luck, a visible path beneath the feet. It is, of course, rather helpful to spot diagonally sliced saplings or neatly severed branches, a sure sign someone has passed by and has used a machete. Game trails further add to the confusion but, generally, can be distinguished from human trails in that they meander and are narrower.

There is a distinct, though faint, reflectivity off the ground where humans have trod. It takes some getting used to to see, but it is definitely there. This glarelike effect is especially noticeable after a light rain or drizzle when a perceptible difference can be detected between the actual path and the vegetation that borders the path. Additionally, with practice, one can appreciate the slight difference in how leaves have curled or "turned" on a path when compared to undisturbed leaves.

Compass and Land Navigation

In the jungle setting, navigation with a compass for a distance of more than 200 yards is fraught with hazard. Travelers who have only a compass should not attempt to cut overland if lost, inexperienced, or on their own unless a significant landmark is visible or sounds of humans or domesticated animals, indicating a settlement, are clearly heard. If, in addition to a compass, the traveler has a GPS unit and knows the precise coordinates of various locations of human habitation, one can travel to the desired destination using the best combination of favorable terrain and distance.

Travel Through Mangrove Swamps

Contrary to what virtually all wilderness and survival books say, you *can* travel through red-mangrove swamps. The prop root system of red mangroves is strong enough to support the weight of any adult. By carefully choosing handholds, great distances can be covered over the roots with minimal effort.

The downside to mangroves is the lack of fresh water and, in many regions, the hordes of ferocious mosquitoes.

Getting Out by Rivers and Streams

Rivers are the jungle's highways. Travel by river is usually the best way to get out and to find help.

Raft   A raft may be constructed by lashing logs together with rope or tough, pliable jungle vines. Balsa trees (*Ochroma pyramidale*), encountered throughout much of Amazonia, make the best rafts. Balsa is often found growing alongside rivers and has the following characteristics: tall, columnar trunk with branches and leaves bunched at the top, which gives the tree a "skinny" look; beige or gray-beige trunk; bark that is smooth but tends to flake, giving it a mottled appearance; and broadly heart-shaped, more or less three-lobed leaves. The key feature of balsa is its remarkably light weight.

Bamboo is light, strong, exceptionally buoyant, and can be used to construct a first-class raft. First, cut down 6 stalks of bamboo approximately 8 to 10 feet long. Next, notch out windows on opposite sides of each section of bamboo near each end. Now, run a sturdy pole through the windows which have been lined up, and lash securely with rope or vines.

A raft constructed in this manner should float for several days. Although you may be able to get away with one row of poles lashed

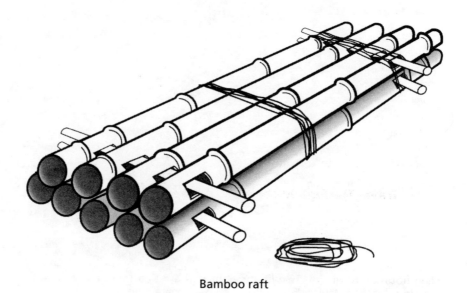

Bamboo raft

together, you will get better buoyancy using two tiers with five poles on the bottom and four on top. Because movement of the sections will eventually break the bindings, it is best to coil up 20 yards or so of additional lianas for use when the original bindings wear out.

Log Flotation Device A log flotation device may be fashioned by using two balsa logs or other lightweight wood placed approximately 2 feet apart and tied together.

Brush Raft A "brush" raft may be constructed by placing buoyant vegetation within clothing or a poncho. Dry leaf litter ("duff") or plants such as water hyacinth may be used as stuffing.

Donut (poncho/tarpaulin) Raft Although not an ideal conveyance for people, a donut raft, also known as a poncho or tarpaulin raft, can be used for transporting equipment across a lake or deep stream. A circle (approximately 3 to 4 feet in diameter) of stakes is dri-

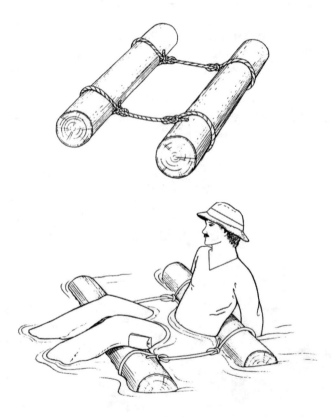

Log flotation device. **A,** Two lightweight logs are tied together to create the log flotation device. **B,** Log flotation device in action.

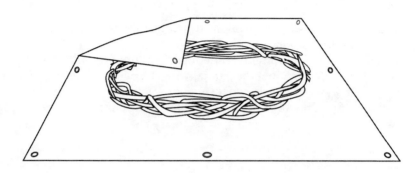

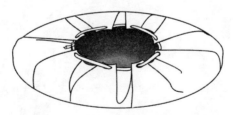

Donut raft

ven into the ground. Pliable saplings are constructed outside the circle of stakes to form a 6- to 8-inch thick hoop framework. Lianas or rope are wrapped around the saplings and knotted in several places to maintain the hoop shape. The hoop is then lifted up from the circle of stakes and placed on a waterproof poncho or lightweight tarpaulin. A rope or long vine is threaded through the grommets and tightened in a drawstring fashion to leave a 2- to 3-foot opening on top. By this means a donut shaped raft is produced that is just right for floating clothing or equipment across a body of water.

POTABLE WATER

It is important to remember that while you can live up to 3 weeks without food, you will not survive much longer than 3 days without water. Fortunately, water is usually easy to find; you are, after all, in the *rain*forest.

Water from creeks and larger streams can be made safe by boiling or using chemical disinfectants such as Potable Aqua tablets.

Drinkable water may be found in lianas, often called "water vines," throughout jungle regions. Vines that contain water are fairly easy to identify because they tend to resemble the "grapevines" of North American forests and have rough, scaly bark. These vines may be several inches thick and contain surprising amounts of crystal-clear water. Vines that do not contain drinkable water tend to have a smoother bark and when cut exude a sticky, milky liquid. Travelers should *not* drink from vines that contain milky or yellow, latexlike sap; these vines are poisonous. When testing for safety of water from vines, first allow a few drops to fall onto the palm of the hand. If no stinging

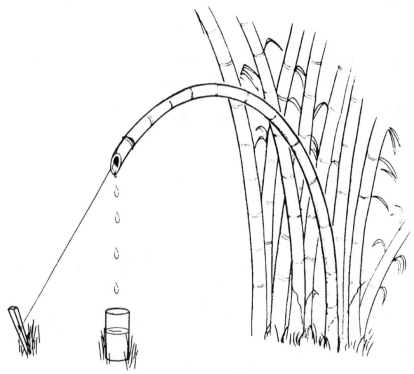

Bamboo as a water source

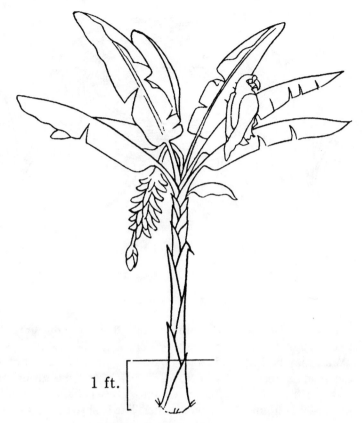

Banana plant as a water source

sensation occurs touch the liquid with the tongue, then taste. If a burning sensation of the mouth does not occur, the water is generally safe.

Maximal amounts of water can be collected from water-bearing vines if the *first cut is made high on the vine* and the second cut is lower on the vine near the ground. After drinking for a while, when the water stops flowing, cut approximately 6 inches from the opposite end and water will start to flow again.

Water may be trapped within sections of certain types of green bamboo. Bamboo that contains water makes a sloshing sound when shaken. Water also may be obtained from green bamboo stalks by bending a stalk over, tying it down, and cutting off the top. Water dripping from the severed tip can be collected in a container during the night.

Large amounts of water can be found in the voluminous natural cisterns formed by the cuplike interiors of epiphytes (air plants) such

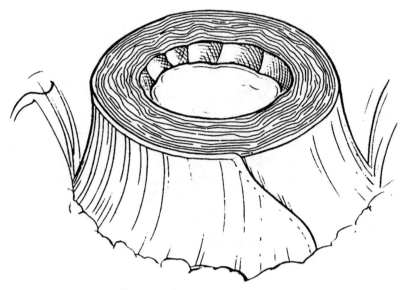

Banana plant as a water source

as bromeliads. The water obtained from these plants should be strained through a cloth.

Water may be collected from a banana or plantain plant by cutting the plant approximately 6 to 12 inches above the ground and scooping out the center of the stump into a bowl shape. The hollow thus formed fills immediately with water. The first two fillings have a bitter taste and must be discarded. The third and subsequent fillings are drinkable. A banana plant can furnish water in this fashion for several days.

The milk of the young, green coconut is an excellent source of liquid and food. The milk of mature coconuts has a laxative effect and should be avoided. Survival guides usually recommend husking the fibrous hard shell that covers each nut by driving a sturdy, long stake into the ground and splitting the husk open by banging the coconut against the end of the stake (which has been sharpened to resemble an ax blade). There is a much easier and safer method: vigorously pound the pointed end of the coconut repeatedly against a big rock; after a couple of minutes the husk splits and can be peeled off exposing the desired nut.

FINDING FOOD

Food is readily available in inhabited regions. Even abandoned villages yield enough fruit and vegetables on which to survive.

Plants

Plants, the most abundant form of food, have the added advantage of being the easiest to procure: plants don't flee when approached and require no particular skills, stealth, or cunning to catch.

Bananas (*Musa* species) and the large "cooking banana," the plantain, are ubiquitous throughout the tropical world. These treelike herbaceous plants have many uses: their fruits are edible raw, boiled, baked, or fried; the leaves can be used to wrap other foods for cooking or storage; and as previously noted, water can be obtained from the plant stump by making a "banana-well."

Root crops such as taro, yams, and yucca should be sought. Taro (*Colocasia* species) is distinguished by large heart-shaped or arrowhead-shaped leaves that grow at the top of a very short, vertical stem; the petiole (leaf stalk) joins the leaf *inside* the leaf margin. Taro can be differentiated from poisonous elephant ear plants in that taro leaf tips point down, whereas elephant ear leaf tips point up. Taro also must be distinguished from poisonous *Caladium* plants; taro has all green leaves, but *Caladium* leaves are brightly colored and patterned. Do not eat taro raw; all varieties must be boiled or roasted to break down the irritating crystals in the plant. Although the tuber at the base of the stem is usually what is eaten, all parts of the plant are edible.

Yams (*Dioscorea* species) are vining plants that creep along the ground and are characterized by heart- or arrow-shaped leaves and square-shaped vines in cross section. The edible tubers can be huge, weighing many pounds, and should be boiled before eaten.

Yucca (*Manihot* species), also known as cassava or manioc, is a staple crop throughout much of Central and South America and tropical Africa. This erect shrub has a straight slender stalk that grows to heights of 3 to 9 feet with deep green, fingerlike leaves. In food preparation, the bark of yucca roots should be peeled off, then the root should be shredded or pounded and boiled to release the toxic compounds they contain. As an extra precaution, the wet pulp should be flattened into a "pancake" and cooked on a grate to drive off any remaining volatile hydrogen cyanide gas.

Ferns are abundant in tropical regions. The coiled, new leaves (fiddle heads) can be eaten raw but are better cooked as a vegetable. The fuzzy hair that covers the tops of fiddle heads can be removed by rubbing or washing. The young shoots of most species of bamboo can be eaten raw or cooked.

Many varieties of palm encountered throughout the tropics have edible hearts. Cut the tree down and remove the new leaves (fronds); the delicious palmheart is located where the new leaves emerge from the top of the tree. The peach palm, *Bactris gasipaes* is a tall, domesticated plant whose palmheart and fruit mesocarp are greatly prized by natives. Finding a peach palm means an inhabited or recently abandoned village is nearby.

Common plants such as the pineapple, mango, and papaya are easily identified. Always wash the hands after handling fresh green papayas; the milky sap of the unripe fruit is highly irritating if rubbed into the eyes.

Edibility Test The military has worked out an ideal Universal Edibility Test to help the survivor avoid unfamiliar plants that are potentially toxic to eat or touch. Unfortunately, this test requires 24 hours to determine the safety of a single potential food item. In a jungle survival situation, where the goal is to get out as quickly as possible, the Universal Edibility Test is just too time consuming to be of much practical use. The following abbreviated version of the Universal Edibility Test draws heavily from John Wiseman's popular *SAS Survival Guide* and the U.S. Army's *Survival: FM 21–76*. These recommendations come into play if you find yourself in the rare survival situation where you can't recognize any familiar plant, have been unable to capture minnows, crayfish, and insects, and, for whatever reason, cannot walk out or expect prompt rescue.

Never eat mushrooms and avoid unknown plants that have:

- Milky or discolored sap.
- Beans or seeds inside pods.
- Bitter or soapy taste.
- "Bitter almond" or peach scent.
- Tiny barbs on the stems and leaves that could irritate the mouth and digestive tract.

If you are driven by necessity to test an unknown plant for survival, make sure you choose a plant that is abundant in the area. First, inspect the new plant, then crush a small portion; if it smells of bitter almonds or peaches, discard it. Check for skin irritation by squeezing some juice onto the inner portion of the upper arm; if discomfort, a rash, or swelling occurs, discard the plant. Next, proceed through the following steps, waiting *15 seconds* between each to see if there is any reaction and discard if discomfort is felt:

- Place a small portion on the lips.
- Place a small portion in the corner of the mouth.
- Place a small portion on the tip of the tongue.

- Place a small portion under the tongue.

- Chew a small portion.

Swallow a small amount and wait *5 hours*. Drink or eat nothing else during this period of waiting. If, after 5 hours have passed, there is no soreness of the mouth, excess belching, nausea, vomiting, or abdominal pains, the plant may be considered safe.

Animals

All mammals, birds, freshwater fish, turtles, snakes, and lizards are edible but should be cooked first to eliminate parasites.

Tiny minnows and crayfish can be found in most tropical creeks and are an excellent source of protein. Minnows can be herded into the shallows and scooped up in a hat or mosquito netting. Crayfish, resembling diminutive clawed lobsters, will be found under small rocks and are easy to capture.

Insects, the most abundant life form on earth, are rich in fat, carbohydrates, and protein (insects are 65 to 80 percent protein, beef is 20 percent protein). As previously noted in Chapter 9, palm grubs, raw or roasted, are a great delicacy (Honest!). In Central and South American jungles, look for trunks of palm trees that have been previously felled by natives who plan to return to harvest the larvae that have developed in the pith. A rotting palm trunk lying on the ground with large areas chopped out by a machete or ax is a sure sign the locals are using palm grubs as a food cache on hunting and fishing trips. Ants and termites are found in rotting logs and in nests. The large, 10-inch-diameter hairy spiders of the Amazon Basin are delicious when properly prepared: singe off the barbed hairs, then roast in the embers away from the hottest part of the fire.

A few caveats on eating insects: 1) avoid any that have a bad smell or produce a rash if handled, 2) remove the legs and wings from larger insects before eating, 3) avoid brightly colored caterpillars and insects, 4) beetles and grasshoppers with hard outer shells may have parasites and should be cooked before eating, 5) avoid "hairy" caterpillars.

So, let's review the case to be made for eating insects in a survival situation: they are abundant, loaded with nutrients, and easily caught. What more could you ask?

Worms (*Annelidea*) are an excellent source of protein and can be found in damp soil or crawling on the ground after a rain. Worms can be cleaned out by dropping them into water for a few minutes (they will automatically purge themselves), or by squeezing them between the fingers. Worms can be eaten raw or dried in the sun and made into a paste. The giant earthworm of the Neotropics is so huge it can be mistaken for a snake; great to eat, great for fish bait. (Do not confuse the tropical caecilians—limbless amphibians—with the giant earthworm. Unlike earthworms, caecilians have jaws and teeth, and for all the world look like blind, purple-gray snakes.)

It is virtually impossible to kill game without firearms. In inexperienced hands, traps and snares are not effective. Much better results are obtained from fishing, or better still from plants and insects.

Mangrove Swamp as a Source of Food

Mangroves are excellent places to forage for food—go in, get what you want, then retreat to higher ground. Mangrove swamps are an excellent place to find snakes (usually nonpoisonous) and bilvalves such as mussels and oysters, all of which make satisfactory eating in a survival situation. The snakes will generally be found sunning themselves atop the prop roots just above the water. Mussels and oysters can be broken off the roots and opened with a knife blade. Use caution when handling bivalves; they can cut like a razor. If one has fishing gear and bait, it is fairly easy to obtain food from the waters at the edge of a red-mangrove swamp; just make your way out onto the roots to where the water is 1 to 4 feet deep, drop your baited hook to near the bottom, and haul in the fish and saltwater crabs.

EMERGENCY SHELTER

Abandoned, temporary shelters previously constructed by natives on hunting and fishing expeditions often have become home to aggressive biting spiders, stinging ants, and snakes. It is usually preferable to take the time to set up a new camp.

In an emergency it is possible to construct a proper shelter using only plant materials. Be sure to clear underbrush and dead vegetation from the shelter site and avoid erecting a shelter beneath dead standing trees and limbs. In a tropical savanna setting where there are trees, poles may be required as vertical supports. In the tropical rainforest, straight and stout trees can almost always be found separated by just the right distance to lash horizontal platform frame poles or, if need be, one or two trees can be used in combination with a vertical pole than has been driven into the ground. A shingled covering can be made quickly and easily from long, broad banana or heliconia leaves laid bottom to top.

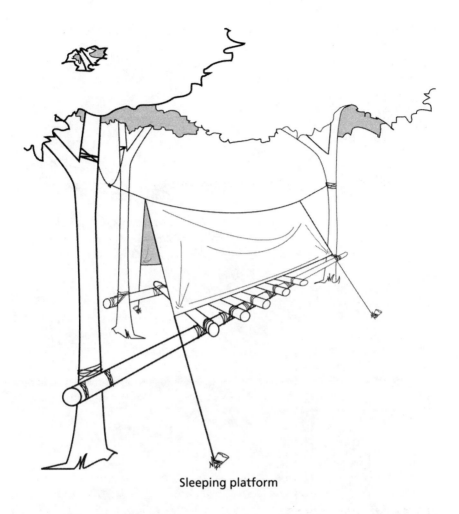

Sleeping platform

Tropical palms provide a more substantial roof but require more time and skill in construction. Select a suitable ground-hugging species or chop down a slender tall palm (palm trees with spines on the trunks often provide the best fronds) and separate each frond into halves. This is accomplished by grasping the frond at the end opposite the base, separating the leaves as though parting hair down the middle, and with a quick jerk splitting the frond in two. The halves should be overlapped like shingles laid bottom to top, then secured to the roof framework.

It is much easier to construct an adequate shelter using a tarpaulin draped over a rope or vine stretched between trees or poles.

Lean-to shelter

MAKING FIRE

In addition to boiling water for drinking and cooking food, fire lifts the spirits, warms the body on uncomfortably cool jungle nights, and can be used to signal rescue aircraft.

Tinder and Kindling

Strips of Tire   There is nothing better suited for making fire in the jungle than little strips (⅛" × ½" × 4") of rubber tire and a butane lighter. *Pieces of car tire will always burn even when wet.* Ray Mears, an expert on survival in any geographic and climatic setting, always carries several small strips of tire and a butane lighter in his survival kit when trekking in the rainforest.

Kapok   The majestic kapok tree, also known as the silk-cotton or ceiba tree (*Ceiba pentandra*), found originally throughout the American tropics and now spread to West Africa and Southeast Asia, produces hundreds of thousands of seeds each year. For the fire-maker this is very good news because each seed is surrounded by cottonlike fibers, known as kapok, which immediately catch fire and make an ideal tinder.

Palm Fiber   The clothlike fibrous material at the base of palm fronds makes an excellent tinder.

Bamboo Fire Saw

If you don't have a butane lighter handy but do have access to bamboo, you can make your own bamboo fire saw:

    1.   With your machete, cut a 3- to 4-foot long section of bamboo.

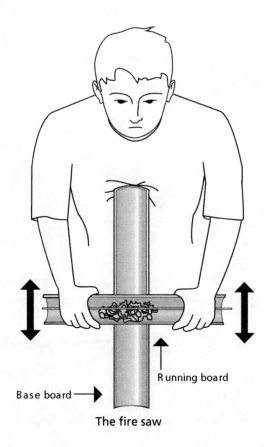

Running board

Base board ➔

The fire saw

2. Split the section the long way with the machete. One of the resulting long sections will be the "baseboard."

3. Shorten one of the split sections to approximately one foot in length. This section will be the "running board."

4. With the machete blade, prepare tinder by scraping the outer sheath of a piece of bamboo. You need one large handful of scrapings.

5. Cut a narrow notch at 90 degrees on the outer (convex) side of the running board so that it just breaks through to the inner wall. This will serve as a guide to slide the running board rapidly over the baseboard.

6. Fill the running board with the scrapings to form a fluffball of shavings.

7. Place a thin strip of wood or a strip of bamboo over the ball of tinder to hold it in place.

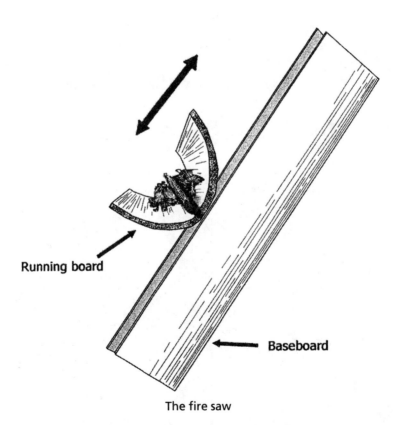

Running board

Baseboard

The fire saw

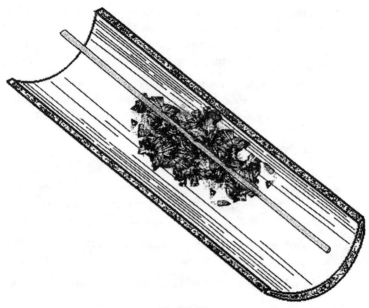

Fluffball

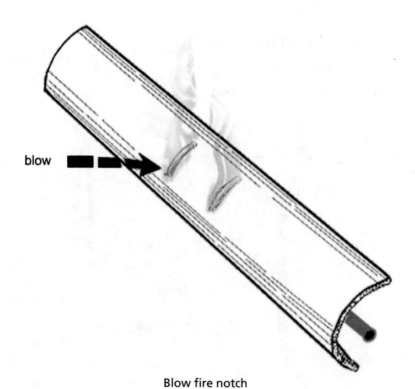

blow

Blow fire notch

8. Anchor the long section of bamboo (the baseboard) with one end in the ground or against a rock or solid log and the other end wedged firmly against your abdomen. The sharp edges of the baseboard should be facing upward.

9. Holding carefully on to each end of the strip of wood that is keeping the tinder trapped inside the running board, rapidly and vigorously slide the running board up and down the baseboard with the grove against the sharp edge of the baseboard.

10. You will know that you are exerting sufficient effort to generate enough friction to ignite the tender when you feel nearly exhausted, have worked up a sweat, and begin to entertain thoughts such as, "This just isn't worth it."

11. As soon as wisps of smoke begin to billow up from the tinder, gently blow upon the tinder until it bursts into flame.

12. Add small pieces of kindling and avoid smothering the fire.

Using this or any other friction method for making fire is hard work, but it *can* be done.

MAKING COOKING UTENSILS

Bamboo Container

Large diameter bamboo makes a great "pot" for boiling water.

Bamboo container for boiling water

To prepare a bamboo cooking pot, take a section of bamboo cut just past each end joint; notch out an opening by making cuts at 45 degrees near each end; run the machete blade between the notches; pop out the "plug." Support each end of the bamboo pot on stakes or sturdy Y-branched sticks that have been driven into the ground.

Palm Spathe Container

No bamboo handy? No problem! Find a nearby palm with a sturdy, woody spathe (the durable, canoe-shaped structure that encloses flowers and fruits of palms). Support the spathe at each end over a low fire and fill the vessel with water. A palm spathe container will stay intact long enough to cook items such as crawfish and minnows.

PSYCHOLOGY OF SURVIVAL

For travelers reared on movies and novels depicting the horrors of the Amazon, there is a built-in overlay of dread with respect to being lost or stranded in the jungle.

Visible daytime threats—the myriad plants bristling with razor-sharp spines, noxious insects, heat, and humidity—are worsened with the onset of darkness. It is during the night that the mind falls prey to distortions of perception. Things unseen transform and magnify: the unsettling, lingering roar of the howler monkey sounds like a jaguar is near, ready to pounce; a remote cascade of water striking hollowed-out rocks becomes the ominous moan of childhood ghosts. No wonder one hears accounts of individuals held in the grip of "woods shock": otherwise rational beings incapacitated by fear to the point of throwing away the very items that would aid in their survival or even fleeing (or attacking) would-be rescuers.

STRATEGIES TO INCREASE SURVIVOR CONFIDENCE

Having survival skills is important; having the will to survive is essential.

Survival FM 21–76

Previous Jungle Experience

It is helpful to begin tropical excursions in the structured setting of small-group travel. Jungle tours, particularly in Costa Rica, Ecuador, and Peru (three countries with a long history of catering to ecology-minded travelers), offer a combination of rainforest trekking, cross-cultural experience, and a heightened sense of the jungle as an ecosystem of beauty and relative safety.

Survival Manuals

Survival manuals, particularly those written by military experts, provide insights gained over decades of experience. The Department of the Air Force manual *Survival: AFPAM 36–2246* is an exceptionally comprehensive reference work on survival. *Aircrew Survival: AF Pamphlet 64–5*, a condensed version of *AFPAM 36–2246*, is small enough to carry in expedition gear and contains useful text and illustrations on shelters, starting a fire, signaling and recovery, navigation and position determination, travel hints, and water and food procurement. *Survival: FM 21–76*, a U.S. Army survival manual, is another excellent source of reliable, time-tested information.

General Reading

Articles and books on the flora and fauna, including human inhabitants, of the tropical rainforest should be read before traveling to jungle regions. Familiarity with exotic plants and animals lessens the likelihood of fear of that which is alien, while increasing one's awareness of their potential utility in a survival situation. The anthropological literature is replete with first-person accounts by anthropologists who have lived under trying circumstances with minimally contacted tribal populations throughout the tropics.

Courses in Wilderness-oriented Skills

Several courses in wilderness survival are offered in the United States each year. NOLS, the National Outdoor Leadership School (307–332–5300, e-mail *www.nols.edu*) teaches wilderness-oriented skills and leadership in a core curriculum stressing safety and judgment, leadership and team work, outdoor skills, and environmental studies. Peter Kummerfeldt's wilderness and outdoor safety courses (*www.outdoorsafe.com*) teach both the psychological and the physiological aspects of surviving a wilderness emergency.

ONE LAST PIECE
OF ADVICE . . .

Having read this book and perused other recommended readings, you should have a general sense of what you may encounter when traveling in the tropical rainforest. You have learned strategies that will help you cope with the wilderness jungle environment, maximize pleasurable experiences, and, if all hell breaks loose, improve your chances of survival.

Wilderness travel is much like off-shore sailing: there are a thousand and one reasons to not get past the thinking and planning stage. Don't be like the vast majority of pleasure sailors who dream of cruising to far-off shores in their little pocket yachts but can't bring themselves to slip the ties to land. The ones who make substantial trips at sea go even when the boat is not 100 percent ready (it never is); those who stay at dockside collecting impressive growths of marine algae and barnacles on the boat's hull always seem to have several projects that must be completed prior to setting sail.

If you have dreams of venturing beyond the familiar and safe world of ordinary vacation travel, commit yourself fully to the undertaking, plan as best as you can, and then simply *go.* I put great stock in Goethe's famous assertion:

> *Whatever you can do,*
> *Or think you can, begin it.*
> *Boldness has power, and genius,*
> *And magic in it.*

Good luck in your travels!

REFERENCES

CHAPTER ONE: GENERAL PREPARATIONS

Auerbach P., Donner H., Weiss E. *Field Guide to Wilderness Medicine*. St. Louis: Mosby, 1999.

Berthoz A., Pozzo T. Head and body coordination during locomotion and complex movements. In Swinnen S.P., Heuer H., Massion J., Casaer P., eds., *Interlimb coordination: Neural dynamical and cognitive constraints*. New York: Academic Press, 1994, pp. 147–65.

Box B., ed. South American Handbook. Lincolnwood, IL: NTC/Contemporary Publishing Group, 2000.

Clement, G., Pozzo T., Berthoz A. Contribution of eye position to control of the upside-down standing posture. *Exp Brain Res* 73(3):569, 1988.

Denslow J., Padoch C. *People of the Tropical Rain Forest*. Berkeley: University of California Press, 1988.

Emsley M., Sandved K. *Rain Forests and Cloud Forests*. New York: Abrams, 1979.

Forsyth A., Miyata K., Landry S. *Tropical Nature*. New York: Touchstone, 1995.

Kennedy B. *Caring for Children in the Outdoors*. Oakland, CA: Adventure Medical Kits, 1994.

Matthews D., Schafer K. *Beneath the Canopy*. San Francisco: Chronicle Books, 1999.

Mazrui A., ed. *General History of Africa Series* (UNESCO). Berkeley: University of California Press.

McIntyre L. *Amazonia*. San Francisco: Sierra Club Book, 1991.

McIntyre L. *Exploring South America*. New York: Clarkson Potter, 1990.

Kritcher J. *A Neotropical Companion.* Princeton: Princeton University Press, 1997.

Schultes R.E., Hofmann A. *Plants of the Gods.* New York: McGraw-Hill, 1979.

Schultes, R.E., Raffauf R.F. *The Healing Forest.* Portland: Dioscorides Press, 1990.

Schultes R.E., Raffauf R.F. *Vine of the Soul.* Oracle, AZ: Synergetic Press, 1992.

Schwerdtfeger W., ed. *World Survey of Climatology,* 16 vols. New York: Elsevier Scientific, 1969–1986.

Silcock L. *The Rainforests: a Celebration.* London: Barrie & Jenkins, 1990.

The Emerald Realm: Earth's Precious Rainforests. Washington, D.C.: National Geographic Society, 1995.

Walden J. *Jungle Travel and Survival.* In Auerbach, P., *Wilderness Medicine.* St. Louis: Mosby, 2001.

Walls J.G. *Jewels of the Rainforest—Poison Frogs of the Family Dendrobatidae.* Neptune City, NJ: TFH Publications, 1994.

Weiss E. *A Comprehensive Guide to Wilderness and Travel Medicine.* Oakland, CA: Adventure Medical Kits, 1997.

Wolfe A., Prance G.T. *Rainforests of the World: Water, Fire, Earth and Air.* New York: Crown Publishing Group, 1998.

CHAPTER TWO: MEDICAL PREPARATIONS

Auerbach P., Donner H., Weiss E. *Field Guide to Wilderness Medicine.* St. Louis: Mosby, 1999.

Dickson M. *Where There Is No Dentist.* Palo Alto, CA: Hesperian Foundation, 1983.

Donner H. Common expedition medical problems. *Wilderness Medicine Letter,* Vol. 17, No. 3, 2000.

Donner H. Expedition medical kit. World Congress on Wilderness Medicine. Wilderness Medical Society. Whistler. 1999.

Iserson K.V., ed. Position statements. Wilderness Medical Society, Point Reyes Station, CA, 1989.

Rose S. *International Travel Health Guide.* Northampton, MA: Travel Medicine, Inc., 2000.

Zell S., Goodman P. Wilderness Preparation, equipment and medical supplies. In Auerbach P., *Wilderness Medicine.* St. Louis: Mosby, 2001.

CHAPTER FOUR: CULTURAL AND PSYCHOLOGICAL FACTORS

Berga S., Mortola J., Girton L., et al. Neuroendocrine aberrations in women with functional hypothalamic amenorrhea. *J Clin Endocrinol Metab* Vol. 68, No. 2, 1989.

Chagnon N. *Yanomamö: The Fierce People.* New York: Holt, Rinehart and Winston, 1977.

Chagnon N. *Yanomamö: The Last Days of Eden.* San Diego: Harcourt Brace Jovanovich, 1992.

Ciba Foundation Symposium 49. *Health and Disease in Tribal Societies.* New York: Elsevier, 1977.

Denslow J., Padoch C. *People of the Tropical Rain Forest.* Berkeley: University of California Press, 1988.

Descola P. *The Spears of Twilight: Life and Death in the Amazon Jungle.* New York: The New Press, 1996.

Diamond J. *Guns, Germs, and Steel.* New York: W.W. Norton & Company, 1998.

Forsyth A., Miyata K. *Tropical Nature.* New York: Touchstone, 1995.

Kirchhoff P. The Caribbean lowland tribes: the mosquito, sumo, paya, and jicaque. In Steward J., ed., *Handbook of South American Indians. The Circum-Caribbean Tribes.* Vol. 4. New York: Cooper Square Publishers, 1963.

Guanipa C. *Culture shock.* Edweb.sdsu.edu/people/CGuanipa/cultshok/.

Harner M. *Hallucinogens and Shamanism.* New York: Oxford University Press, 1973.

Howell N. Surviving fieldwork. *American Anthropological Association,* No. 26, 1990.

Lizot J. *Tales of the Yanomami.* Canto edition. New York: Cambridge University Press, 1991.

Metraux A. Religion and Shamanism. In Steward J., ed., *Handbook of South American Indians. The Comparative Anthropology of South American Indians,* Vol. 5. New York: Cooper Square Publishers, 1963.

Oberg L. *Culture Shock and the Problem of Adjustment to New Cultural Environments.* Worldwide Classroom, *www.adventuresabroad.com*

O'Connor G. *Amazon Journal: Dispatches from a Vanishing Frontier.* New York: Dutton/Plume, 1998.

O'Hanlon R. *In Trouble Again.* New York: Vintage Books, 1990.

Robarchek Clayton, Robarchek Carole. *Waorani: The Contexts of Violence and War.* Fort Worth, TX: Harcourt Brace, 1998.

Schultes R.E. *Primitive Plant Lore and Modern Conservation.* New York: Orion, Summer, 1988.

Schultes R.E. *Hallucinogenic Plants.* Racine, WI: Golden Press, 1976.

Schultes R.E., Hofmann A. *Plants of the Gods.* New York: McGraw-Hill, 1979.

Thomsen M. *Living Poor: A Peace Corps Chronicle.* Seattle: University of Washington Press, 1997.

Willey G. Ceramics. In Steward J., ed., *Handbook of South American Indians. The Comparative Anthropology of South American Indians,* Vol. 5. New York: Cooper Square Publishers, 1963.

Whitten N. *Sacha Runa: Ethnicity and Adaptation of Ecuadorian Jungle Quichua.* Urbana, IL: University of Illinois Press, 1976.

Yen S. Reproductive strategy in women: neuroendocrine basis of endogenous contraception. In R. Roland, ed., *Excerpta Medica Amsterdam,* 1988, pp. 231–239.

Yost J. Twenty years of contact: the mechanisms of change in Wao (Auca) culture. In Whitten N., ed., *Cultural Transformations and Ethnicity in Modern Ecuador.* Urbana, IL: University of Illinois Press, 1981.

Yost J. People of the forest: the Waorani. In Gordon-Warren P., Curl S. *Ecuador: In the Shadow of the Volcanoes.* Quito: Ediciones Libri Mundi, 1981.

CHAPTER FIVE: DYNAMICS OF GROUP TRAVEL IN EXOTIC ENVIRONMENTS

Beck A. *Love Is Never Enough.* New York: Harper Perennial, 1989.

Belloc H. *The Cruise of the Nona.* New York: Hippocrene Books, 1983.

Cameron D. Deep freeze. *The Sydney Morning Herald,* October 16, 1999.

Cashel C. Group dynamics: implications for successful expeditions. *Journal of Wilderness Medicine* 5, 163–170, 1994.

Cashel C., Lane S., Montgomery D. Emotional response patterns of participants during a wilderness experience. *Wilderness and Environmental Medicine* 1, 9–18, 1996.

Collins D. Psychological issues relevant to astronaut selection for long-duration spaceflight. AFHRL Technical Paper 84-41, Government Document, 1985.

Eisendrath S., Lichtmacher J. Psychiatric disorders. In Tierney L., McPhee S., Papadakis M., *Current Medical Diagnosis and Treatment.* Stamford, CT: Appleton & Lange, 1999.

Erb B. Predictors of success in wilderness ventures. *Wilderness Med Lett,* 7(3), 8, 1990.

Hackett P. Personal communication.

Harrison A., Connors M. Groups in exotic environments. In Berkowitz L., *Advances in Experimental Social Psychology.* New York: Academic Press, 1984.

Hollander E. *Leadership Dynamics.* New York: The Free Press, 1978.

Houston C. Personal communication.

Houston C. Who will you take on a high mountain expedition? *Wilderness Met Lett,* 7(3); 11, 1990.

Hubbard J., Franco S., Onaivi E. Marijuana: medical implications. *American Family Physician,* December 1999.

Jordan D. Group Dynamics. In Jordan D., *Leadership in Leisure Services.* College Station, PA: Venture Publishing, Inc., 1996.

Law P. Personality problems in Antarctica. *The Medical Journal of Australia* Vol. I, No. 8, 1960.

Monz C. An analysis of the medical review process at the National Outdoor Leadership School. *Wilderness and Environmental Medicine* 8; 130–47, 1997.

Petzoldt P. *The New Wilderness Handbook.* New York: W.W. Norton and Co., 1984.

Phipps M. Group dynamics in the outdoors. In Cockrell D., ed., *The Wilderness Educator.* Merrillville, IN: ICS Books, 1991, pp. 35–64.

Sandal G., Ragnar V., Ursin H. Interpersonal relations during simulated space missions. *Aviation, Space, and Environmental Medicine* Vol. 77, No 7, 1995.

Schultes R.E. Primitive plant lore and modern conservation. New York: Orion, Summer 1988.

Stark F. *A Winter in Arabia.* Woodstock, NY: Overlook Press, 1987.

Sullivan A. The he hormone. *The New York Times Magazine,* April 2, 2000.

Tuckman B. Developmental sequence in small groups. *Psychological Bulletin* Vol. 63, No. 6, 1965, 384–399.

Ward M. *High Altitude Medicine and Physiology.* London: Chapman and Hall Ltd, 1989.

Wood J. A comparison of positive and negative experiences in Antarctic winter stations.

Wood J. Pyschological changes in hundred-day remote Antarctic field groups.

CHAPTER SIX: UNDERSTANDING YOUR SURROUNDINGS

Beebe W. *Tropical Wild Life.* New York: New York Zoological Society, 1917.

Couzin J. The forest still burns. *U.S. News,* April 19, 1999.

Denslow J., Padoch C. *People of the Tropical Rain Forest.* Berkeley: University of California Press, 1988.

Ehrlich P., Wilson E. Biodiversity studies: science and policy. *Science,* Vol. 253, 16 Aug. 1991.

Emsley M., Sandved K. *Rain Forests and Cloud Forests.* New York: Abrams, 1979.

Evans D. Personal communication.

Forsyth A., Miyata K. *Tropical Nature.* New York: Touchstone, 1995.

Goulding M. Flooded forests of the Amazon. *Scientific American,* March 1993.

Kricher J. *A Neotropical Companion.* Princeton: Princeton University Press, 1997.

Lovejoy T.E. Foreword. In Forsyth A., Miyata K. *Tropical Nature.* New York: Touchstone, 1995.

Lovelock J. The ages of Gaia. New York: Bantam Books, 1988.

Marsh G., Bane L. *Life Along the Mangrove Shore.* Hobe Sound, FL: Florida Classics Library, 1995.

Meggers B. *Amazonia: Man and Culture in a Counterfeit Paradise.* Washington, D.C.: Smithsonian Institution Press, 1996.

Myers N. *The Primary Source.* New York: Norton, 1984.

Nadkarni N. Canopy roots: convergent evolution in rainforest nutrient cycles. *Science,* Vol. 214, 27 Nov. 1981.

Nicholaides J., Brandy D., Sanchez P., et al. Agricultural alternatives for the Amazon Basin. *BioScience* V. 35 No. 5, May 1985.

Perry D. Life above the jungle floor. New York: Simon & Schuster, 1986.

Petrick C. The complementary function of flood lands for agricultural utilization. *Applied Sciences and Development* 12:26–46, 1978.

Ramsay C. Mosaic of life. In *The Emerald Realm: Earth's Precious Rainforests.* Washington, D.C.: National Geographic Society, 1995.

Raven P. Endangered realm. In *The Emerald Realm: Earth's Precious Rainforests.* Washington, D.C.: National Geographic Society, 1995.

Richards P., Baillie I., Walsh R. *The Tropical Rain Forest.* New York: Cambridge University Press, 1996.

Sanford R. Apogeotropic roots in an Amazon rain forest. *Science,* Vol. 235, 1987.

Schimper A. *Plant-Geography Upon a Physiological Basis.* W.R. Fisher, transl. P. Groom & I. B. Balfour, eds. Oxford, Eng.: Clarendon Press, 1903.

Shukla J. Amazon deforestation and climate change. *Science* 247:1322–1325, 1990.

Simberloff D. Mass extinction and the destruction of moist tropical forests. *Zh. Obshch. Biol.* 45:767–778, 1984.

Skole D., Tucker C. Tropical deforestation and habitat fragmentation in the Amazon: satellite data from 1978 to 1988. *Science* Vol. 260, 25 June 1993.

Stark N., Jordan C. Nutrient retention by the root mat of an Amazonia rain forest. *Ecology* 59(3), 1978.

West R. *The Pacific Lowlands of Colombia.* Baton Rouge: Louisiana State University Press, 1957.

White P. *Nature's dwindling treasures: rain forests.* Washington, D.C.: National Geographic, Jan. 1983.

Wilcox B. In situ conservation of genetic resources. In McNeeley J. and Miller K., eds., *National Parks, Conservation and Development: The Role of Protected Areas in Sustaining Society.* Washington, D.C.: Smithsonian Institution Press, 1984.

Wilson E. *Biodiversity.* Washington, D.C.: National Academy Press, 1989.

Wilson E. *The Diversity of Life.* Cambridge, MA: The Belknap Press of Harvard University Press, 1992.

CHAPTER SEVEN: COPING WITH THE JUNGLE ENVIRONMENT

Auerbach P. *Medicine for the Outdoors.* New York: The Lyons Press, 1999.

Goodman P., Kurta K., Carmichael J. Medical recommendations for wilderness travel, *Postgrad Med* 77(8):173, 1985.

Kaplan L. Suntan, sunburn, and sun protection. *Journal of Wilderness Medicine,* Vol. 3, No. 2, 1992.

Sauer G., Hall J. *Manual of Skin Diseases.* Philadelphia: Lippincott-Raven, 1996.

Watts K., Mulder G. Heat illness. In Richmond J., Shahady E. *Sports Medicine for Primary Care.* Cambridge, MA: Blackwell Science, 1996.

CHAPTER EIGHT: JUNGLE TREKKING

Fleming P. *Brazilian Adventure.* New York: Scribners, 1934.

Fleming P. *One's Company.* New York: Scribners, 1934.

Hansen E. *Stranger in the Forest.* Boston: Houghton Mifflin, 1988.

O'Hanlon R. *In Trouble Again.* New York: Vintage Books, 1990.

Parker T. *Lighthouse.* New York: Taplinger, 1976.

CHAPTER NINE: CAMP LIFE

Descola P. *Spears of Twilight.* New York: New Press, 1996.

Dufour D. Insects as food. *Am Anthropologist* 89(2):383, 1987.

Schultes R.E., Raffauf R.F. *The Healing Forest.* Portland: Dioscorides Press, 1990.

Weatherford J. *Indian Givers.* New York: Crown, 1988.

CHAPTER TEN: HAZARDS REAL AND IMAGINED

Schreck C. Protection from blood-feeding arthropods. In Auerbach P., *Wilderness Medicine*. St. Louis: Mosby, 1995.

Bettini S. *Arthropod Venoms*. New York: Springer-Verlag, 1978.

Berault J. Candiru: Amazonian parasitic catfish. *J Wilderness Med* 2(4):312, 1991.

Suchard J., Connor D. Scorpion envenomation. In Auerbach P., *Wilderness Medicine*. St. Louis: Mosby, 2001.

Davidson T. Snakebite protocols. *www.surgery.ucsd.edu.ENT/DAVIDSON/snake*.

Dyott G.M. Manhunting in the jungle. New York: Blue Ribbon Books, 1930.

Esslinger J. Arthropods other than insects. In Beaver P., Jung R., *Animal Agents and Vectors of Human Disease*. Philadelphia: Lea and Febiger, 1985.

Forsyth A., Miyata K. *Tropical Nature*. New York: Charles Scribner's Sons, 1984.

Graham D. Tear gas and riot control agents. In Haddad L., *Clinical Management of Poisoning and Drug Overdose*. Philadelphia: Sanders, 1990.

Guderian R. Personal communication.

Boyer L., McNally J., Binford G. Spider bites. In Auerbach P., *Wilderness Medicine*. St. Louis: Mosby, 2001.

Holldobler B., Wilson E. *The Ants*. Cambridge, MA: Belnap Press of Harvard University Press, 1990.

Kricher J. *A Neotropical Companion*. Princeton: Princeton University Press, 1997.

O'Hanlon R. *In Trouble Again*. New York: Vintage Books, 1990.

Reid H. Spider bites and venomous stings. In Maegraith B., Gilles H., *Management and treatment of tropical diseases*. Oxford: Blackwell Scientific Publications, 1971.

Stewart R., Burgdorfer W., Needham G. Evaluation of three commercial tick removal tools. *Wilderness and Environmental Medicine* 9: 137–142, 1998.

Use S., Tieszen M. Cutaneous myiasis from *Dermatobia hominis*. *Wilderness and Environmental Medicine* 8: 156–160, 1997.

Wirtz R., Azad A. Injurious arthropods. In Strickland G.T., *Hunter's Tropical Medicine*. Philadelphia: Saunders, 1991.

Wymper E. *Travels Amongst the Great Andes of Ecuador*. London: Charles Knight and Co., 1972.

CHAPTER ELEVEN: HEALTH RISKS TO TRAVELERS

MacKenzie W., Hoxie N., Proctor M., Gradus S., et al. A massive outbreak in Milwaukee of cryptosporidium infection transmitted through the public water supply. *The New England Journal of Medicine*, July 21, 1994.

Ansdell V.E., Ericsson C.D. Prevention and empiric treatment of travelers' diarrhea. *Med. Clin. N. Am.* 83: 945–73, 1999.

Centers for Disease Control and Prevention. *Health Information for International Travel 1999–2000*, Atlanta, Ga.: DHHS.

Figueroa-Quintanilla D., Salazar-Lindo E., Sack R., et al. A controlled trial of bismuth subsalicylate in infants with acute watery diarrheal disease. *N. Engl. J. Med.* Jun 10; 328(23):1653–8, 1993.

Jong E. Travel medicine. In Auerbach P. *Wilderness Medicine*. St. Louis: Mosby, 2001.

The Medical Letter On Drugs and Therapeutics: Advice for Travelers, Vol. 41 (Issue 1051), April 23, 1999.

Rose S. International Travel Health Guide. Northampton, MA: Travel Medicine, Inc., 2000.

CDC (*www.cdc.gov/travel/*) Information for health care providers: Malarone for malaria treatment and prophylaxis. Updated October 27, 2000.

Tierney L.M., McPhee S.J., Papadakis M.A. *Current Medical Diagnosis and Treatment*. Stamford, CT: Appleton & Lange, 1999.

W.R. Weiss, et al. *J Infect Dis* 171:1569, 1995; D.J. Fryauff et al., *Lancet* 346:1190, 1995.

CHAPTER TWELVE: WOMEN IN THE JUNGLE

CDC web site: *www.cdc.gov*

Cook G., ed. *Manson's Tropical Diseases*. London: Saunders, 1996.

Fleming A. Haematological diseases in the tropics. In Cook G., *Manson's Tropical Diseases*. London: W.B. Saunders, 1996.

Kummerfeldt P. *www.outdoorsafe.com*.

Kovacs G., Rusden J., Evans A. A trimonthly regimen for oral contraceptives. *The British Journal of Family Planning* 19: 274–75, 1994.

Linsay S. Effect of pregnancy on exposure to malaria mosquitoes. *Lancet* Vol. 355, June 3, 2000.

Manning A. Women face mosquito menace. *USA Today*, June 2, 2000.

Mortola J., Buchsbaum G. Women in the wilderness. In Auerbach P., *Wilderness Medicine*. St. Louis: Mosby, 1995.

Rose S. *International Travel Health Guide*. Northampton, MA: Travel Medicine, Inc., 2000.

Sulak P., Cressman B., Waldrop E., Holleman S., Kuehl T. Extending the duration of active oral contraceptive pills to manage hormone withdrawal symptoms. *Obstet Gynecol* Feb; 89(2):179–83, 1997.

CHAPTER THIRTEEN: TRAVELING WITH CHILDREN IN THE TROPICS

Bemelmans L. *My Life in Art*. New York: Harper Brothers, 1958.

Centers for Disease Control and Prevention. *Health Information for International Travel 1999–2000*. Atlanta, Ga.: DHHS.

Drugs for parasitic infections. *The Medical Letter on Drugs and Therapeutics* Vol. 40 (Issue 1017), January 2, 1998.

Goodyer L., Behrens R.H. Short report: the safety and toxicity of insect repellents. *Am. J. Trop. Med. Hyg.* 59(2), 323–24, 1998.

Howell N. Surviving fieldwork. *American Anthropological Association* No. 26, 1990.

Kennedy B. *Caring for Children in the Outdoors*. Oakland, CA: Adventure Medical Kits, 1994.

Klein J., Kennedy B. *Children in Wilderness*. In Auerbach P., *Wilderness Medicine*. St. Louis: Mosby, 2001.

Neumann K. *Travel with Children*. World congress on wilderness medicine. Whistler, British Columbia: Wilderness Medical Society, 1999.

Weiss E. *A Comprehensive Guide to Wilderness and Travel Medicine*. Adventure Medical Kits, 1997.

CHAPTER FOURTEEN: INFECTIOUS DISEASES

Beaver P., Jung R. *Animal Agents and Vectors of Human Disease*. Philadelphia: Lea & Febiger, 1985.

Benenson A., ed. *Control of Communicable Diseases Manual*. American Public Health Association, 1995.

CDC Fact Sheet. Cyclopsora infection, *www.cdc.gov*.

Chin J. *Control of Communicable Diseases Manual*. American Public Health Association, 1999.

Cook G., Manson P. *Manson's Tropical Diseases*. Philadelphia: Saunders, 1996.

Core Curriculum on Tuberculosis: Division of Tuberculosis Control, Center for Prevention Services, Centers for Disease Control, and the American Thoracic Society. June 1990.

Preston R. Crisis in the hot zone. *The New Yorker*, October 26, 1992.

Preston R. *The Hot Zone*. New York: Random House, 1994.

Rose S.R. *International Travel Health Guide*. Northampton, MA: Travel Medicine, Inc., 2000.

Shaw R.A. The reactive arthritis of giardiasis. *JAMA*, Vol. 258, No. 19, 20 Nov. 1987.

Snyder J., Blake P. *Is Cholera a Problem for U.S. Travelers? JAMA* Vol. 247, No. 16, 1982.

Strickland G.T., ed. *Hunter's Tropical Medicine*. Philadelphia: W.B. Saunders, 2000.

Tierney L.M., McPhee S.J., Papadakis M.A. *Current Medical Diagnosis and Treatment*. Stamford: Appleton & Lange, 1999.

CHAPTER FIFTEEN: SURVIVAL STRATEGIES

Aircrew Survival: AF Pamphlet 64–5. Department of the Air Force, 1985.

Craighead F., Craighead J. *How to Survive on Land and Sea*. Annapolis, MD: Naval Institute Press, 1984.

Dufour D. Insects as food. *American Anthropologist*, June 1987.

Lansing A. *Endurance: Shackleton's Incredible Voyage*. New York: The Adventure Library, 1994.

Leach J. *Survival Psychology*. Basingstoke, Eng.: Macmillan, 1994.

Mears R. Ray Mear's Extreme Survival, *Jungle*. BBC Television Documentary Film, 2000.

U.S. Air Force Pamphlet 64–5: Aircrew Survival. Washington, D.C.: Dept. of Air Force, 1985.

U.S. Air Force Regulation 64–4: *Survival Training,* Vol. I. Washington, D.C.: Dept. of Air Force, 1985.

U.S. Army FM 21-76: Survival. Washington, D.C.: HQ Dept. of Army, 1992.

Wiseman J. *SAS Survival Guide*. Glasgow: HarperCollins, 1993.

INDEX

nighttime fears, 179
Nix shampoo, 20
no-see-ums, 27, 29, 33

O'Connor, Geoffrey, 53
O'Hanlon, Redmond, 110
oral rehydration salts (ORS), 78, 79, 81,
    129, 141
organizer bags, 34

palm spathe container, 179
pants, 27
parasites, 127, 130–31, 142–43, 155–56,
    171
Parker, Tony, 89
Peace Corps, 124
pens, 34
People of the Tropical Rain Forest
    (Denslow & Padoch, eds.), 8
Pepto–Bismol, 19, 128
Permethrin, 20, 33, 103, 132, 133
Perry, Donald, 66
Peru, 5, 65, 99, 179
photography, 8–9, 36–38
physicians, 13–15, 114, 129, 130, 132,
    133, 148
pillows, 32
piranha, 110
pith helmets, 26
plague, 17
plants
    ant "protectors" of, 102–3
    dangerous, 88, 116–17
    as food, 96–97, 169–71
    water from, 166–68, 166–68, 169
    Plants of the Gods (Schultes &
        Hofmann), 8, 48
plates, 31
pocket tools, 34
poison-dart frogs, 111
polio, 17
political unrest, 13, 26, 118–20
poly bottles, 34
ponchos, 27
porters, 6, 43, 48, 78, 85–86
potable water, 98–100, 166–68, 166–68
Prance, Ghilean, 8
pregnancy, 137–38
Preston, Richard, 154, 155
prickly heat, 80
pullovers, 26

rabies, 17, 111
rafts, 163–65, 163–65
Rain Forests and Cloud Forests (Emsley),
    9
rainforests
    mangrove swamps, 70–71

saturation-humidity cloud forest, 69
super-humid, 65–69
tropical savannas, 69–70
Rainforests: A Celebration, The (Silcock), 8
Rainforests of the World (Wolfe &
    Prance), 8
rainy season, 3, 9–10, 59, 75, 118, 140
razors, 34
readings, 7–10
Reid, H. Alistair, 109–10
repatriation. See reverse culture shock
reptiles, 112–18
rescue situations, 159–61
respiratory infections, 19
reverse culture shock, 41–42, 52
River Blindness, 155
rivers, 26, 30, 109–10, 117, 118, 140
    diseases and, 151
    rafts, 163–65, 163–65
    trails and, 161
Robarchek, Clayton and Carole, 45
Rose, Stuart R., 145
roundworm, 155

SafeWater Anywhere, 118
salmonella, 127
SAM Splint, 20, 115
sandals, 25
Sandved, Kjell B., 9
sanitation, 98–99, 125
SAS Survival Guide (Wiseman), 170
satellite images/phones, 158–59
savannas, 69–70
sawgrass, 86–87, 117
Sawyer Extractor, for snakebite, 115, 116
scabies, 20, 142
Schafer, Kevin, 9
schistosomiasis, 124, 125
Schultes, Richard Evans, 8, 48
Schwerdtfeger, Werner, 10
scorpions, 106–8, 142
sexuality, 16, 46, 56, 60–61, 136
shamanism, 45–46
shavers, 34
shelter, 91–94, 172–73, 173–74
shigellosis, 150–51
shirts, 26–27
Shuar Indians, 48, 114
Silcock, Lisa, 8
sinusitis, 19
skin problems, 14, 76, 80, 82–84, 119, 137
Skin So Soft (SSS), 33
smoke signals, 160
snakes/snakebite, 18–19, 24, 111, 112–16,
    142, 172
soap, 30
socks, 26
Sodium Sulamyd, 20